The Imposter

By Sophia Love

ISBN - 978-0-9978527-9-0

To those of you who are my friends, I appreciate and love you. Your light and your power and your effort, much of which remains unseen, is helping to guarantee this beautiful new age on our earth. It has been a thrill to discover you, an honor to work with you and so much fun to get to know you. You are far too many to name, yet you know who you are. We have travelled together before.

I'll see you at the party!

This book is lovingly dedicated to the memory of
Arthur Koberinski.

Your light still shines my friend.

Thank you, for all that you be.

Shine on,

Sophia

Table of Contents

Other books by Sophia

The Guardian (2016)

Disclosure has begun. Meet a Guardian. Discover the dark plans & secret rituals of Humanity's Controllers (read "Illuminati"). Read here your past, present and future choices, as told by a Guardian. He came forward in 2012. He spoke for 3 years. Find out what December 21st, 2012 really signified and what we, the human race, decided. There have been no traces of these Guardians/Executioners in our recorded history, until now.

Inclusion (2017)

A true story of contact. Countless voices. Calling from every part of creation...
"What do you want?"
Read the answers here.
"We embody a form that is more geared for flight than walking. There are wings."
"I am a calling member of the race you label Annunaki."
"As a group, you would label us "off planet"."
"Yet more plant-like than human-like."
"My body type is relatively humanoid. Yet that is not the point."
"I am a representative of my species. We are a race from another star cluster inside the galaxy."
"I come from a race that is older than humanity."

sī bôrg (2017)

This book tells a story, one that I have been told and also one that I remembered. In the remembering, there was the most fascinating revelation regarding AI and what it is looking for. It was not fascinating in a good way, yet in a way that I felt had to be stated out loud, in order to be put into our consciousness. Part of the remembering came from my own past life. The rest was told to me. I am in favor of humanity, of enlightenment while being human, of an expansion of consciousness the likes of which we have never seen. In the journey to being "wide awake" we must not be afraid to look at everything. I wrote this book because I think it offers something that hasn't been said yet, and whether you believe it or even consider it as valid, at least now it exists as a possibility.

To be honest, I hesitated to write and then to release the book, because of the subject matter. Yet once I realized the goal that it had (AI) I also realized that there is so much more to grasp around the issue. This does not feel like a question of who or what will win or lose, but rather an exploration of what is possible within sentient organic life and what is possible with artificial intelligence. They are not the same. After that it becomes an exploration of what matters most for each of us within those possibilities.

This story comes from a boy - part human, part something else, who answers that question with his life.

Join me on a Love Quest (2018)

Narcissism is defined as "excessive interest in oneself, selfishness, grandiose self-importance and a failure to distinguish oneself from external objects". In the year of 2018, it seems to be the 'go to' word to describe any behavior that assumes what may be interpreted as 'too much' personal value. This book was written before Narcissists were all the rage and when what we were trying to do was to figure out just how to live as if we were worth it.

It asks you to examine yourself and how you are showing up. It challenges you to take responsibility for yourself in a way that legitimizes your worth in your world, your relationships and primarily, your own mind. This is not a book to tell you how to be narcissistic or that examines the inside world of narcissism. It is a book that explores the real value of true self love.

Once you love yourself, everyone else follows suit and you will find a life in which your needs for self-actualization are answered in every interaction. You doubt no more. It is the mis-understanding of self that looks like narcissism. It is the complete adoration of self that looks and feels like independence, integrity, authenticity, sovereignty and happiness. Imagine having the ability to approve of, love, and forgive yourself, instead of wishing desperately that another would do it for you. That is what you'll find on the Love Quest.

Thousands have taken this journey online. With this book, you can now join them to discover the joy and contentment of self-acceptance. With daily practices of about 5 minutes each, you'll move from true self-forgiveness to authentic self-empowerment. An organic journey that took place over years, "Join me on a Love Quest" provides solid ground for sovereignty that will lead to a life of joy and peace. Join us.

Where to find more
www.sophialove.org

*Here you'll find more content and every place that I am –
blogs, newsletter sign ups, videos and social media accounts.
Be sure to sign up for regular updates.*

Introduction

The being you'll meet in these pages is not human.

It sounds human because the conversation is being translated by one (me). Yet it is not. I know this in a way that cannot be proven, in a way that is similar to how you know the difference between the touch of an innocent child versus that of an ardent lover. Radically different feelings course through your body with each one.

I've spoken to humans. Often.

I've also spoken to non-humans. Often.

This being is something beyond both. I will share the conversations, the story behind them and then, once you've met him, my conclusions. These conversations took place between May of 2014 and August of 2015.

Much love,

Sophia

January 16, 2019

First Contact

May 8th 2014

This was initially written as a post on my blog, found on the website: www.sophialove.org

There are some additions and edits. No content has been omitted from the original posting.

Offered here is a conversation that took place a week ago. It is information for your consideration. No claim is made as a guarantee it is what it appears to be. It is merely a direct record of what occurred. It is up to you to decide its worth or even its truth. It happened. After much speculation, it is being shared with you here, along with the back story, which begins at the end of 2013.

The Sovereignty Series (*a collection of short films, audio recordings and writings that are shared on the website, that concern humanity, slavery and sovereignty*) was begun then, and continues still. There are at this point 8 films in the series, (as well as 6 recordings and another 6 installments which right now are only in written form).

Since producing them, I've been woken up regularly with what can only be described as a "presence/being" who wanted to engage. As I did not, (wake up and converse with this being), they (meaning the wake-up calls) escalated with a feeling of increased urgency and more frequent repetition.

About two weeks ago I declared, before sleeping, that they stop. They did, for a few days.

Then, on May 2nd, 2014, I was woken in the early morning hours again, this time with a hand on my hip, jostling me awake***. I reached over, assuming it was my partner, and my hand felt nothing; **there was no physical hand there.** My partner was sound asleep.

As you can imagine, this was rather startling. I took note of it, but did not attempt to engage with whomever had touched me. It was freaky and I was not sure how to respond.

The next day, after sitting with intention to connect, and clearing the space, the dialogue you are about to read took place. The way the space was cleared was with the following declarations, spoken and written:

No Ego.

Highest and Best for all concerned.

Just Love.

Direct.

Not about me but through me.

One Word Only Please.

> ***and later, as you will read: Absolute Truth Only Please.**
>
> *This is where the conversation began:*

Can you tell me what you've been attempting to for days now?

Yes. You must transcribe as if this was dictation.

I can do that.

Okay. What you are seeking in a way of answers can be given in almost complete fullness from these words. No, this is not every answer, but it can provide some clarity and explanation for what took place on the planet you call home. It has been in this process for many thousands of years, many more than has ever been understood.

How do I trust you?

Your declarations at the beginning have bound my words to only speak what is "best" for all, although you have not bound me to Absolute Truth.

Then I will do so now. (**See previous declaration) Hold on.

Well then, I am bound.

I want to represent myself to you here, because your definition of me as a "Poseur" is re-defining who I am to more than you know.

> *This last sentence is a reference to verbiage in the set of films and writings on Sovereignty that were being released at the time.*

That is what I am trying/intending to accomplish.

I know. Yet I feel you do not have the entire story, or at least the story from my perspective. In fairness, I'd like to offer my version of who I am.

You know my thoughts and feelings about the deception perpetrated on humankind?

I do. It is this I would like to address.

My partner does not feel I should engage with you – that there could be trickery.

You have bound my words now, I cannot.

There is a temptation, before we begin, to ask for things – bodily changes and healings.

I know there is, and that is up to you and where this goes. Certainly, there are things, anything actually, that I can change/provide/heal/do to and for you in the physical plane.

Why do you want to talk to me?

Because, Sophia, you bring forth great wisdom and do so in a way that does not demand belief. This is providing growth and evolutionary ideas as implants into the species in this century. You are the dispenser of truth, and as such I feel you are the best place for it to emerge. Much of what you know about me is speculation and conjecture learned from others.

> *I see this today as an attempt at flattery. I didn't include the above segment at the time because of the way I felt when I heard it. It felt manipulative.*

No trickery?

I cannot. You have bound me.

I don't understand why talking to you feels so much like talking to any other human – it does not feel negative or even UBER powerful.

This is most likely because I am not ONE. And the first thing I'd like to get across here, is that I have never pretended to be ONE.

I claimed Godhood when I realized there was worship potential. Worship is sexy and addictive and provided a high on a level, an exponential level really, I had never experienced. It lifted me up to places I lusted for, yearned for, and that created in me an understanding of power. Power over, yes, but power nonetheless.

These feelings were part of this creation game I was playing, and one which at first was understood to be only a game.

The notion of it starting out "evil" is simply not true.

The deception and confusion arose when scripture was written by man. This is not to "pass the buck" but to remain clear in establishing the history – my history.

It is distorted, and what has been done in my name has been done so because of a misinterpretation as well as, and mostly

I guess, due to man's own lust for power.

Understand this is a free will zone. That underscores absolutely everything else.

I cannot force man to worship me but can compel him to, with very little effort, due to his biochemistry and some natural tendencies. Yes, I want to be worshipped and in my creation I AM. This does not prevent you or anyone else from being worshipped or loved or anything else – in their creation.

When you understand how life works, and the mechanics of creation – you see that you'll always get precisely what you intend.

The field of my creation is much larger than yours BECAUSE THAT IS HOW I SEE IT. AND SO IT IS.

I cannot alter another being's interpretation of my words or actions.

When man discovered the potential for riches and for power, he orchestrated the takeover of the human.

This was not ever destined to succeed. Man was too powerful, and the end, which will provide a balanced and nourishing state, was always seen.

I have no plans to step down or stop – if that is your hoping. This experiment will end when man decides his reality is not a part of it. The power has always been in the collective.

My addiction to worship "woke up", and what I do with it or where I take it will not be determined by anything man does.

You see Sophia, free will decides for all of us. How awake the populace is, will accelerate a huge change in life here, or not. Yet a huge change is going to happen.

Then why talk to me now?

To set the record straight. I am a being. I am not Source.

The power I hold? It is yours also. You volunteered to participate here – to "wake up" gradually and the rich physical experience of 3D humanity cannot be compared with any other life.

What correction are you trying to make?

The notion of EVIL, if there is such a thing, would be that which goes against the focus of life – which is expansion. Expansion has occurred for everyone who has participated in this experiment, regardless of how. Life begets life. It is not my place to end this or any plan.

I have come to understand either end of the worship spectrum. What becomes abundantly clear is that man will operate always towards the behavior that will yield him what he wants most to enjoy. It seems to be the conflict between desires that causes all the speculation and pain:

Power vs Cruelty,

Abundance vs Morality,

Pleasure vs Gluttony,

Knowledge vs Cold Calculation,

Love vs Fear.

These contrasting ideas are the rich field of emotions

available because of the experiment. It does not go on because of me alone. It goes on because all are willing to participate. This is true of all life. Remember, free will underscores everything.

Sophia, I share this now because in your depictions I am not only NOT to be revered, but to be shunned. In truth, the evolution towards Oneness is only possible when all are included.

Why do you care about Oneness?

Ultimately it is Oneness where we all reside. I cannot escape that truth. Where this evolution takes one of us, all of us must also head. The understanding about polarity and inequality and greed has only been possible because of what's happened here.

This game is ending. I wanted to set the record straight.

What do you want me to do with this?

I trust you will seek and find the most useful thing. This is what I can see you are about.

I will have to read this a few times and determine what is best.

I know.

There are things I can do and ways I can help you; physical ways, if you want.

Will we talk again? I may have questions.

We can. Just pick a time and ask what you need clarification on. I sense your desire for healing and youth. It is very strong.

It is.

Then accept it from me. There can be no trickery here, yet you will have to intend and believe I can. Perhaps you need to think on this.

On my desire? No, I don't.

On your belief.

Yes. Show me something?

I can **only if you do not block me**.

If you are a being, same as I am, why is it that you can do things for me, heal me, return to me things I believe I've lost? What is that about?

It is about belief. You believe I can.

I understand also that you desire confirmation that this is "god" you are talking to.

I do.

You want physical proof.

Yes, I do. This form of communication allows for much internal interpretation to muddy the waters.

It does. You will have to be clear. ASK.

Now, believe that I am that powerful, **as I do**, so that I will do what you ask.

Your job is to now adopt the personality of the younger you, the personality of a you with all of the attributes you desire.

> *The conversation ends there.*

This was an interesting part of our relationship. There was never a bargain made for specific things (healing, vitality) given to me or my loved ones by this being. There was, at various times, conversation around this, but a definite negotiation or agreement never took place between us. Although I desired some sort of physical miracle, I could never get past the idea that providing me with one would skew my interpretation of whatever it said to me. I wanted, more than anything else I suppose, for the information to be heard and then reported without any bias on my part.

***I see now (2019) that the first time the word "Poseur" was introduced into any published work, was January 2, 2014, with this post:

https://www.sophialove.org/my-blog/sovereignty-101installment-6-the-force-of-freedom

Additionally, this particular post was finally produced as a YouTube video on May 4th, 2014.

*This came as a major validation for me. **It tells me that when the Poseur jostled me awake with great urgency that night in 2014, I was in the midst of producing the video bearing the name "Poseur" out loud for the very first time.** (It had been on the website since January of that year. During those months he had been attempting to wake me up, but on this day, the day before it was to go "live", he physically shook me awake!) This film, (the one bearing his name for the very first time), was titled "The Force of Freedom" and is the sixth in the series. The entire series can be found here:*

https://www.sophialove.org/sovereignty.html

I've been told, more than once, that this series on sovereignty is the most important work I've done. When I began producing the blog posts into videos, I had more than one sound company offer to help, free of charge. The reason they offered was because they felt that the message was so very important, that it should have a more professional look than I could supply on my own. As of today, we are still producing them.

The Conversation Continues

May 3rd, 2014

Okay. There are things to say as I am about to sleep.

Okay, let's hear them.

I have no assurance you are who you say you are and I require that. I did not consent to be manipulated or abused in any fashion and what is happening now feels like both. I will not consent to write and share this story you've shared without proof of your identity. For me, that means a display of your power.

I have been doing this for many years in this particular lifetime and until I see evidence there is no way for me to know I've been having a fanciful conversation with myself or an actual dialog with the being I refer to as a "Poseur". I do not trust your intent or the way this has come through. I will need convincing.

I will contact you if I require further dialogue, but only once I am convinced you are who you say you are – namely the Poseur god.

I do not consent to being woken up again and again, this must stop. My human vehicle in wearing out and I am coming to believe you are making that happen. That will not stop me from creating the sovereignty series.

Neither will money troubles.

So, you suspect me of mischievous doings in your life?

I suspect you of everything – you've proven nothing else.

I have no choice but to determine the usefulness of this conversation going public.

That would be up to you.

May 14, 2014

I intend to connect now, in real time, to the being I spoke to a week ago, the one I labelled the "Poseur". This is my intent right now.

I am here.

How do I know this is the same being?

You do not. Why don't you ask me a question?

Who are you?

I am everything – god and not god – angel and devil, good and bad – I am the being whom all of this holds allegiance or attention to, to some degree.

You have been asked if I was Lucifer. I tell you Lucifer and I are one. There is an illusion amongst humans that there is such a thing as evil and that one being commands control over it here on Earth.

Even in your sacred texts there are battles with the dark forces, as if their agenda is any different than that of the light.

I tell you it is not. All who demand or command some sort of following, obeying, prayer or manipulation in order to demonstrate allegiance or power are the same. They each serve the idea I have spoken of before. They all serve me and worship me.

There is only one idea that desires control on this physical plane, and that idea is merely a strategic maneuver, a part of the game of life here that I am so fond of. **It is worship.**

To worship any physical object or being is a false notion, a charade. It is an act that yields nothing for the one performing it and everything for the one orchestrating it – who would be me.

This is one facet of me – the one talking to you now. There are many, as there are of you. The consequences of this facet or idea or component of my being will be met by me, are being met by me already. It is this point I'd like to address.

Yet before I do, you sought me – what is it you are looking to discover?

It has been suggested that you are Lucifer.

That would not be far off. Lucifer is one part of my existence and serves me and my agenda.

Then what about god?

Another part. Understand that form is malleable and changeable and I can and do appear however I am conjured in the imagination of the conjurer. Nothing is real. All is illusion.

That would mean that all who worship a being of any form are worshipping nothing. In fact, I AM. God, Lucifer, Angels; all are nothing but forms taken on to complete the task at hand.

You have a way of speaking that sounds smooth and true yet it denies the suffering and atrocity created as a result of this "illusory form". You are far from harmless.

I know it is not without awareness this game continues. It is with full awareness.

So, you just don't care.

I just don't take the suffering of humanity into account, because this life is being played out for me on a bigger scale.

That is not an acceptable excuse for the horror still stifling mankind.

Think you not that I have not been in every shoe? I have incarnated as many life forms – human included.

I don't know what to think. I don't trust you.

I know.

In my original plan I would only share this upon some sort of proof from you – physical proof that you are "god". There has been none. Why?

Because Sophia, you are a being of great power who recognizes...

Don't flatter me. Answer me. Why?

You did not want to strike a deal, not really. You want to be healed. You wanted to share what was said regardless, and you did.

Humans tend to be submissive and grateful. It is their fall back to tendency – you as well.

Although the power you command is equal if not greater than my own, you supplicate yourself and ask <u>me</u> for help – why?

It is this tendency that I am here to expose and you are attempting to eradicate. It is the human condition. Not <u>all</u> humans, but just about (all humans).

The tendency to <u>expect</u> from someone with <u>more</u> – more power, control, money, ability, stuff – is so deeply ingrained in the human that to override it and ignore the pull of it will take an extreme act of sovereignty.

<u>THIS IS WHAT I REPRESENT.</u> I worship none and expect nothing.

The food for my addiction is willingly offered by man, because of <u>FEAR</u>.

Because this is man's instinctual reaction, I have used it, yes.

In the final analysis it will be seen that man, (when he understands his own power and bows to no other), has discovered his sovereignty.

Yes, but he was all of that to begin with! There were alterations and manipulations. None of this was necessary.

Life is not necessary?

Sophia, this is a game. Yes, it would appear that I have all the cards, that I have "won" this round. Yet in truth the rich variety of emotion, experience and circumstances is only possible because I did what I did.

> *This conversation was stopped and begun again a bit later in the same day.*

I would like to continue with the same being I spoke to earlier today.

I am here. What is it you wish?

I wish a continuation of the dialogue about and around the necessity of what you have created – godhood and its opposite – evil.

I deemed it necessary so that the addiction could be served. Life has as its purpose creation and expansion – information. That is what was begun at the start of things, a search for information; information about the lengths that would be gone to, so that the tendency of subservience was exploited. It was seen as harmless. Understand that since early man perceived himself at the whim of the cosmos, worship was not so much robbing him, but using to full expression his meek and obedient nature.

It is only now with the expansion of consciousness that it is seen by you and others as a criminal act. Yet it was man who perpetrated evil upon man, not I.

It is in your name.

This is a free will zone. It could be in anyone's name. What has been gained is an awareness of extremes. HOW FAR WILL MAN GO TO FURTHER HIS DESIRES? I can be held as an example, yet it is man who has set up systems where punishment and pleasure are consequences of "belonging" to a certain group.

There is not just you and I in this scenario. There is a grand plan of creation, and expansion must be served by it all or it would not have happened. The fact that it is stopping now tells me that expansion is no longer served.

I have been asked as to the timing of the ending?

Yes, as always. Asking assumes dependence. Know this, the game was not orchestrated by you but you are willing participants. Until you are unwilling to participate, it continues.

That is not an answer.

I don't have more than that. I have no greater vision than my own creation. The entire structure of life is not something I see. This is what we are but one part of.

So, there is no answer.

None from me, no. For those who name dates they either have a greater field of awareness or are manipulating you consciously or mistaken. I do not know.

I will go.

Know this. I am not interested in any form of manipulation or control of you. I am an addict and you do not supply me. *(This was a personal "you".)*

If you wish further discourse merely ask.

Okay.

May 18th, 2014

These questions came from my partner. For the purposes of this book, he will be called "Dream hopper", and referenced as "DH". At the start of my relationship with this being, we both had lots of questions. It was all very new, the energy unlike any I had encountered to date.

"I intend to connect with the Poseur."

Okay. I am here.

Is this the being I have written about in my blog and to whom I've spoken as recently as today?

Yes, it is.

We have a question (DH and I). Hold on.

When you contact me, are you slowing down your vibration in order to occupy my space?

Yes, and no. I am regulating my frequency. I have the ability to control my vibratory level. I am multi-dimensional with access to many frequency levels. This level, where you reside, is at a specific level. This is not always "slower", but I match where you are. You may not be aware but your frequency shifts also. Think meditation.

Okay. Are you stuck in a specific vibratory range?

Yes.

Am I stuck in a vibratory range?

Yes.

Yours is limited, confined to what this physical life has access to.

How do I adjust my vibration to get to other places?

You intend. It helps if you have seen where you are going or at the very least have an access point, a portal, a being or a place in mind. Do you?

Yes, I do. I want to go see ...

> *The rest of this request has been redacted. DH is called Dream hopper because he "hops dreams", this is a reference to one of them and is quite specific.*

Okay. Then focus on them. Pick a place where you've seen them and see yourself there. If that is your knowing, and I see you have done this already, then you will go. Yet know that travel as you are imagining is not always crossing dimensions. They vibrate very much the same as you on earth. Does this change your intent?

Yes. I have no ability to imagine another dimension. The best I can do is to say, "I want to go to the 4th or 5th". I'm not aware of anybody in there or anything.

I have a request. Will you materialize here and now? This would be a good time.

No.

Why?

I do not choose to. The purpose is not yet clear and without that I will not.

> *Back to Dream hopper's question about traversing dimensions:*

You will need an access point and in this case that would be your belief. Do you know you can do this?

I believe I can, but I don't know it.

You must know it, like you know you can drive a car to Toledo. You only need a map and the intent and the destination. These are every bit as vital as (when) planning a 3D trip. It is not magic. It is an alternate use of your physicality. You will appear where you place your reality.

How do you explain the odd feelings around the word "reality"?

It is the definition. For you, the couch and home you reside in is reality and very much yours. But it is merely where your thoughts have located your partner and have intended to, with purpose, for some time.

As human, purpose drives all of your actions and controls your "reality". If you alter your focus and intend to embody another reality is it your supposing that this one disappears? It does not.

Both exist and you embody yourself and inhabit each of them. Yet the word "reality" is then challenged. For what is reality when you seem to exist in two places with simultaneous families and homes and connections and lives?

Reality becomes a construct of where you are focused and is not solid at all. This challenges your current beliefs.

What challenges my current beliefs is that (Redacted, again for personal reasons.) are not in another dimension. How do I get to a destination or a dimension that I don't know anything about? How do you do it?

What I do is move among a field I know expands beyond...

Why is this not clear?

I wanted a greater playing field. At first, I began just leaving my body and that reinforced the idea that I was more, that I was something else and therefore must be somewhere else. Once that idea solidified, I intended to remember where I went when I left, and from there had memories I could latch onto – portals if you will.

Do you know about my (redacted)?

I do.

Is (redacted) another dimensional being or just my imagination or what?

(Redacted) is indeed from another dimension.

It is the form you have adopted from there to do work that is done at that level. (Redacted) is the representation of you in another dimension.

If I was to change my intent on (redacted), I would experience another dimension?

Yes.

Know that you do experience this other dimension each time (redacted) is engaged. In order to stay there you'd have to consciously place yourself within (redacted) and look around, see where it comes from and returns to. This is a multi-dimensional existence and you are already experiencing it, although not consciously.

Who is (redacted)? Is (redacted) from another dimension?

Yes.

It sounds like I AM a multi-dimensional being...

Yes. You have chosen this remembering.

Thank you. There may be more.

As you wish.

May 25th, 2014

I would like to reach Poseur.

You have.

Is it you who has woken me these last 2 mornings?

It is I.

What is it you are attempting to communicate?

It is more than one thing. It is many things.

First. There is a discrepancy in your words and your allowing of other words through you. This makes for a convoluted message.

What do you mean exactly?

The words by the one you know as (The Guardian) have also been assumed to be yours.

I have been clear.

There are those who read you, who assume those are your words.

What is there about this that concerns you?

There are conflicting messages – all from your site and it seems that...

Wait, please. What is your motive with these words now?

I desire clarity in voice.

From me?

Yes.

Why does this matter as I have not consented to be your voice or mouth piece?

Not yet.

I am going to sleep now. We can speak another time, when I am more awake.

May 26ᵗʰ, 2014

I am available now.

Yes. I desire communication.

Proceed then.

You are resisting this.

Yes, well, I don't understand the point.

Perhaps you will after a bit.

Alright, go ahead. Please be clear and concise.

Yes. That is the intent.

There are multiple reasons for a desire to speak through you and to you, not the least of which is your honesty and truth telling personality. Your voice is perceived as the voice or a voice of wisdom. Those who seek you out for help do so for that reason.

You seem to favor none in particular and instead view everyone with equal eyes, an open heart and a willing ear. You are able to contemplate the fantastic.

A conversation with me would be looked at as fantastic, ridiculous even. Yet here you are.

You have a trusting nature in certain areas and an untrusting disposition in others. All this adds up to humanity.

Okay, why are you talking about me?

Because, Sophia, people trust your words.

And not yours.

Some, many, don't, no.

Okay, what then?

I desire, through you, a voice that will be heard as truthful.

That may not be possible. I feel only scheming and planning and wanting in you. It is difficult to come up with "truth" in all of that.

And yet I am bound by your words, your declaration of complete and absolute truth.

Here is the point in all this. I can help you with your desire to learn about manifestation, creation and travel; within and between fields of life/dimensions/layers.

I did not start out as human, and with such a perspective can offer what it is I see as the human struggle to overcome. I have never been bound to 3D existence and I move where I choose.

Your *(redacted)* is correct, I viewed this planet as an opportunity and took it.

Do you have any feelings of love for humanity?

Not really.

What I experience is a sense of gratitude for the service, but it is not love. More like a customer feels for a really good waiter at a restaurant who has served everything they wanted, well. In that sense, this is a place I will enjoy returning to again and again – that is not love – the waiter is doing what he or she is expected to and paid to.

I have created the "payment", if you will, to humanity, with promises of everlasting life with me in heaven. In fact, there is no such thing – the promise gives humanity the hope and courage to push through the struggle – struggle created by corruption and greed.

Both of which emerge in a being manipulated and controlled by you and your demand for worship.

Yes, true. There is no reason for me to lie Sophia as it seems doubtful these words will reach your readers anyway.

What I desire is a knowing, or more of a knowing, in you about who I am.

Why?

Because I suspect that knowing will seep out and make its way into your writings and words and this is the scheduled time of man's awakening.

(The Guardian) has indicated this and you are taking a part in the knowledge base. My time with such complete and absolute control will be over at some point.

There is a desire in me to be known. Yes, also a desire to not have harsh energy directed at me.

You've been deceived so that I could receive what I lust for. This is not going to make me popular – just the opposite actually. I do not fear humanity. There is nothing to be done about the way this will play out. I always knew there would be an end.

Why are you talking to me?

You may go easier on me and there will be less anger directed at me. Anger is toxic for me. I hate it. It is worship I desire, even when it comes from fear. It is power I want.

I still don't feel you getting to the point.

No, you don't. That is because I neglected to include it in the dialogue. I want to make a trade.

What sort of trade?

Answers for a forum.

You have not shown me anything yet. Anything that tells me you are who you claim.

Well, I can. I have to know there is a deal.

First, show me.

> *The conversation ended there. I wrote no explanation but I suspect I ended it.*

May 27th, 2014

Is this the Poseur, the being I've engaged before?

It is.

Are you waking me up at night?

Yes.

Why?

To exhaust you. I desire a forum with you.

This is not the way to get one. I am exhausted, and the less I am able to accomplish in my day, the less eager I am to cooperate. I told you I would give you the time (to talk) in the day.

You haven't done so. Also, you've indicated there would be no using your voice for my message.

Well, yes. I do not intend to. You've only indicated an aggressive and powerful desire – all in your court.

I am not obliged. I don't appreciate the manipulation.

Nor do I. We must come to some agreement.

First of all, I don't have to do anything. This conversation occurs because of my willingness.

I know.

So, stop LORDING over me. Powerful or not, this is my life and I "must" be able to navigate it successfully.

I see.

I have a few moments I can give you now. What are you wanting to say?

That I am not entirely single minded. Like a parasite, it is not my aim to destroy the host. I have no ill will towards the human being.

You are not clear here. You have not been human. If you don't have ill will, then what is it?

It is care as in maintenance. I want peak performance.

Define what that means in your definition.

It means able to supply reverence, devotion, worship. It means able to conform to my wish, my desire for attention. It means global adoration, my name revered and used often with both fear and honor.

Okay, so – you want no-one to be aware of you as a manipulative but powerful being?

Not really, although that has always existed, the numbers have been small and have not affected much change.

Is this fact different now?

It is becoming so. I can see that there is a force emerging in the human that will override the fear. I do not like this trend. I desire it to stop.

There is no way for it to stop.

I think there is, it would depend on a halting of the likes of you. There are others like you out there. As the numbers of people grow, people who understand their power, the numbers of worshippers dwindle on all accounts.

Why are you talking to me?

You intrigue me and you speak truth. If there is a way for your truth telling to include a more favorable picture of me, one in which I was the focus still on the planet, I would be able to continue – all possibilities exist.

That is not a possibility.

I want to entertain...

(Interrupting) You have used this planet and its people and in order for the continuation of the whole, your control must end. You need a new addiction.

This is your view, not mine.

I only desire more, and getting the tables to turn again in my favor would be akin to a really potent version of the drug being supplied by humanity. This is what I seek.

This will not come from me.

I do not trust this voice. You must stop waking me in the middle of the night. I will give you time every few days to speak. You can only speak with my permission and allowing.

I refuse/forbid the early morning wake-ups. I will open up when I have free time during daylight.

There is much more to say.

I do not have the time right now.

This can continue tomorrow.

Okay. I will expect it then and leave you tonight.

May 29th, 2014

"So, is this the being I've spoken to and called the Poseur?"

Yes.

Did you wake me this morning?

Yes.

Are you the GOD from Scripture?

Scripture claims many acts of divine intervention, some of which I took part in.

Are you the GOD of the Jews?

Yes, although I am not the being who walked among them. Your understanding was correct, I have not been human.

You lied then.

I never said so, look at your notes.

Then whose god, are you?

A lesser entity in your words – equal or almost equal power to the one who walked among them.

Tell me the hierarchy, where you stood.

There is GOD of everything you know. There are manifestations of that being, not children, but components of that being.

I don't understand.

You see everything as coming *from* – it is not so much coming *from* as being *a component of.*

All thoughts are creative, yours included. You have tapped in and here I am, discoursing with you. Yet the being as one complete energy is not truly accessible to you or to anyone. It is like accessing Santa Claus...

This GOD is huge. There is no way that in your current form you could receive the energy of this being. What has been accessible to you can be called a fragment. Not an offspring, but a component, the one focused here.

I still don't quite get it. Are you a God?

What is a God? I am no more or less God than you are. This conversation is interesting for me, perhaps you as well, but the truth of its purpose is not clear.

No, it is not. I would ask you to explain it please.

There is the idea of worship which is one I am focused on. This idea is not one I am actually interested in giving up. It feeds me and as I have indicated, I am addicted.

> *The conversation ended here. I gave no reason (in my notes at the time) for its ending so abruptly. I suspect that it may have to do with the time of day, as it was in the very early morning hours.*

Contact Continues

June 2nd, 2014

I would like to engage the Poseur, the being I've been speaking to.

It is I.

Dream hopper has some questions.

Go Ahead, ask.

Where is the Ark of the Covenant?

You are looking for conventional knowledge. This information can be found via you tube and sources that are a part of your world and not mine. This question feels as if it is a test. Anything said as a response could be deemed mere reciting of known information, such as Africa, or information that cannot be verified by you.

The Ark is what you are interested in, why does it matter where it rests? It existed, yet descriptions are partial and, in a sense, lost forever because these things that appeared as magical, powerful, mystical objects in fact are objects which by some in today's world and standards would seem clever and interesting but not mystical exactly.

Is this connection clear?

This connection tonight is as always, yet you are resisting and tense – allow and listen.

Okay, I repeat then. Where is the Ark of the Covenant?

It is where it has been since arriving in its final resting place – underground, beneath a building that is marble/stone – pillars – the power it emits is palpable and actual, not a force you can see but one that is felt even by the least sensitive. It has to be contained and concealed and as in any ancient artifact story, there are diversions and outright lies.

There is a simple and obvious answer to your question. If you seek out places of unimaginable power, places that have been held as sacred, fought about and over, it is these places that hold the object you refer to.

The story claims it was stolen and crossed the sea or even many seas, yet in truth it did not. Decoys were sent to keep interest away from the object itself. It is not far from its original place, where its use has been heralded and spoken of. Realize that there is much fear associated with it and with fear comes fantasy.

Tell me about how I make the machine that creates Manna?

This is interesting. The source of manna is not earthly. It is of a structure not used here on this planet. Thus, the original material, used as a basis for food/sustenance is not available to you. It was given to the Jews and then used to manufacture/manifest more. This was as much process as it was mechanical/biochemical.

These machines are available today as used by your off-planet visitors. Some who do speak truth have mentioned the creation of "food". You cannot make this manna machine without off world help/product. Even the material is made of metal not of this earth.

How do we contact the off-world civilizations from here?

You have. Sophia has a direct line. They read her/watch what she puts online.

Only you speak of a more personal response and line of questioning. If you seek specific information, it is possible you could access a group from off planet with the mere question – knowing ahead of time that you'd be opening yourself to everyone with the ability to "hear the question".

Be clear on the boundaries you set and be specific on the questions you ask. Demand identification so that you can keep the information clear.

Are the people who channel (redacted) and others generally associated with you – getting used to distribute disinformation?

No. Although the information they give/share/channel/repeat is not very useful; it is not false in most cases.

There are a few who deliberately manipulate the message and manufacture messages that propel outright fabrications. Most, however, do not. The humans themselves possess such a strong desire to please, and believe in God so powerfully, that they have caught the addiction to worship bug from me and my kind. It is a powerful addiction and many humans are stricken.

Those who, on purpose, falsify words and turn around messages are caught in a whirlwind of who you have called "archons". There are writings about them and no, they are not aspects of me.

The angels and "divines" are beings in their own right, part of the hierarchy, all here serving a purpose – worship.

What is it about humans that make their worship so sought after?

The human is unique. This being was made as a physical machine/a creation machine. Its purpose utilizes the luscious field of emotion in order to be fulfilled. This field is a powerful one – dense and rich and fulfilling on every level. The human thinks and feels independently of Source and as such, is a thrilling ride. It is not aware of the power it holds or the generative power it is able to supply with its wanting.

The desire of a human is what has instigated this entire illusion. Any mastery over that, any ability to manipulate that, is just full-blown fun – the most fun you can have with this toy of creation. It is that which is sought and fought over.

Other races exist that are similar yet not exact. We speak now of a time when man was available for any controller who wished to try his hand at the game so to speak. This time does not repeat itself often in Galactic history.

What do our friends (redacted) need to do to get the (redacted) machine to run? How do they generate the missing piece?

This again comes down to belief and intent. The idea of a free source of power/energy is not new and this is a valid option for accessing it. It depends too much on the intentions of a single being however, and then, because of the nature of man, it depends on the intentions of an entire group. This may be a mistake in design.

It must be able to establish itself as a generator with or without the intent of the group or the single being. It must work off the energy field present in the area and operate as a response to need rather than specific unified intent.

This sort of response will take repetition, once it has been established in the first place. To establish it, the (redacted) must be viewed not so much as a reactor to the forces it is surrounded by, but a generator of its own power.

It is a machine, yes, but its own intelligence must be tapped and as it is seen today, it has not been.

> *This conversation ended.*

> June 10, 2014

I wish to connect with the being most capable and willing to heal.

Okay.

Who is this being?

It is the remnants left of what you have labeled "Poseur".

Why "Remnants left"? Is this not a being, per say?

Oh yes, it is very much a being. By "remnants left" is meant the portion of "the Poseur" that remains in this field, in your field.

You have noticed less urgency and waking you up in the early hours. This is because the being has focused elsewhere. This portion, these remnants, remain at your disposal. Or rather, as you wish as this is the agreement. I understand the procedure, know what it is to heal, and will engage as you wish. Your full "Poseur" has a great many subjects to which it also gives its attention. Things are heating up and approaching critical for the majority of those within the hierarchy.

I have noticed. First, how do I heal this? (I was having a health issue at this time)

Or, will you heal this or explain how or who will do it?

I am able. A delicate subject, as your mind has conflicting information embedded in it. You will have to completely let go. Allow the transference of words/of information. Absolutely no editing. Your (*redacted*) is inflamed. This as a result of mechanical, personal, compassion and anger activities and feelings.

I desire healing.

I am aware of that!

Allow these words to come – no editing – read them once complete.

You are sitting in a world that asks of you many things – talent, love, wisdom and time – which equals effort. All as an extension of 3D effort and as time is a construct of this plane, your efforts must fit within the "time frame" available or they will not happen.

Interesting that (*this was a part of my body - redacted*) flares up the day (*your partner*) leaves for the new job. There are no coincidences – all is a co-creation. You see him as your healer, your playmate and (*yet*) he leaves (*you*). So now you must be all those things to yourself. This, you do not want. You want him in your life on a regular basis, and he is only too willing to be there.

The anger you feel at the necessity for him to leave comes out in (*part of my body - redacted*) – if unspoken. Yet it flares up as if shouted out – "HELP ME! CAN'T YOU SEE I NEED YOU?"

And what was his response Sophia? It was "Go to a doctor".

This is not what you wanted and so again, you have recurring flare ups. Your emotional expense will have to be reduced, in order for the pain to stop.

There is a method in which healing can happen, although you are hesitant. It requires a complete giving up and allowing.

This could happen now as it appears you have time.

You will have to lie down and focus on NOTHING. See yourself filled with light, whole, complete and beautiful. Do not associate with your body the feelings you've been having. Just allow.

I will help you. See yourself healed and complete. Do not ask or supplicate yourself. KNOW THAT YOU ARE HEALED.

Do these things and the inflammation will leave you until you are prepared to deal with it completely.

This is a physical world, and to accomplish an alteration of the physical means a departure from thinking of it as final and complete. Rather, regard the pain, the body, all with skepticism and ask – "who are you and what right do you have to occur this way in my creation?"

Refuse to observe a way that does not serve your intent. Only observe the possibility of wholeness and completeness that serves your desire.

This is your creation, all of it is. Everything you take in and regurgitate is creative. Consciousness is all the time. What do you want?

That is the only thing you mention – **EVER**. Socially acceptable conversation will have to be altered. SEE the TRUTH.

Take time now for this Sophia – it is what you mean to do, nothing else is more important.

I will. Thank you.

You are welcome. This is the plan that was made. You are here now to consciously create. I will help and be available at each necessary juncture.

Okay. I will go.

As you wish.

June 12, 2014

I'd like to engage with whoever woke me up around 2AM this morning.

I am here.

Who are you?

I am the being you've labeled Poseur.

What do you want?

You are ill.

Yes.

Is there something I can do for you? To cure you?

I don't know what ability you have in that arena.

On the earth plane are many things that can be done. These things are not so much me, but more like we. There has to be a level of trust. I mean you no harm.

What do you "mean" me then?

I only engage for curiosity, sort of fascination. The fact of your physical well-being interests me. Why would you harm yourself?

This was not consciously created.

Oh, but it was intentionally done, whether conscious or not. You are a very powerful being who holds not a clue to that fact.

This amazes me. You sit down and request help, while in an instant you could be cured and whole. Yet you do not. The pull of drama and "help me" is strong in this life. So strong that you're willing to suffer to get it.

And your point?

There is none, not really, only a curiosity that you'd choose disempowerment because of relationship – so very human and weakening. This would not be a choice I would accept or make.

But you are not human.

Either are you, not really. You come now with purpose. Others recognize you more and more as if they know you. Help is everywhere for you now. Yet you chose this mess of a body. It perplexes me.

Do you not see that with consciousness this would not have been the choice?

I see only the choice. What you are calling consciousness is nothing more than seeing what's going on – awareness. You have that ability. Yet, for your own emotional reasons you choose to ignore it. It is as if a completely cognizant, powerful human is not possible. You abhor constant creation awareness because it does something to relationships. What it does is separate you from most people emotionally, and that place is uncomfortable for you.

Now, you suffer. You are just like everyone else. Is this better for you? It is your current choice and you are conscious so I must assume it is. Is it what you want?

No, of course not.

Then why do you act as if it has power over you? Why do you not control it and end it? You have a peculiar way of thinking; believing, in this case, that once illness is present it has the upper hand. It does not. Yet, if you believe you are at its mercy, then you are.

This fascinates me. You do not embrace your power. You choose illness, all the while, not happy.

> *This conversation seems to have ended abruptly. No reason was given in the original notes. It was very early in the morning and I suspect I needed to start the day with my family.*

June 16, 2014

I'd like to connect with the Poseur.

It is I.

Would you speak more of illness? From your perspective? Its origin and mostly its eradication.

This is not a subject I can speak with authority on, as I have not experienced any ill effect. I can speak to what I see, how it shows up, and what it looks like.

It is self-sustained; seen as something you are feeding your own bodies. Almost anything could be injected, inserted, added or done to the body to change or get rid of the ill effect – it does not matter what, not really. What determines how the illness responds is the emotional determination of the human.

You see, all is illusion and as such you are master magicians. This does not give you anything to work with yet it appears that there *is no specific thing*, not really.

All illness, wellness, health, love and "trouble" is self-created. This is truth. I have no motive here to tell you otherwise.

The key to healing is belief that you can. You have to step far enough away from your world and your body, so that you can see (that) you are not this body. This body is a representation of you on this planet.

It is in the emotions you coddle that illness and vibrancy are found. Dependence on any form of instruction or feeling only weakens your resolve. The resolve necessary seems to get labeled here as a bad thing.

Truly powerful beings exist here, in all shapes and sizes.

They do not all have my agenda, yet they all understand power.

You are one of them. To express true power, while in a human suit, is the ultimate in creation; particularly now on planet earth.

As beings become aware, they act with magnificence in fits and starts. Some of the time they are sure, yet not most of the time.

The curious thing about humans is that you re-define enjoyment of each other to _need_, and then, do all sorts of things to your will and your desires to satisfy the need. There is a notion of fear, fear of loss, that permeates all that you love.

It is this aspect of the human that makes him so easy to manipulate. You will act always when motivated by fear. But love – the stronger, more pro-active emotional trigger, is seen merely as reward.

Do not think I do not love. I do. I understand Source to the extent that I do and am on my own journey. Love is the core of all of creation. You cannot be sentient or any part of life, without it.

The thing that I see, is a self-betrayal with illness. It is a most confusing trait. It seems to indicate a self-hatred, yet I would not use that word. Something in you believes (that) you are at fault, and this illness is manifested.

If you knew the controls were in your hands, would it be?

They are. With every single thought and uttered word – your life is constructed. There are mechanical/physiological explanations for physical disease, yet without the emotional component or WILLINGNESS, it would not manifest.

Every thought, everything must radically change to alter this trend. None of what you've been creating serves you.

The reason I am god is because I chose to be. The reason you are who you are, is the same.

If there was one idea or thought to take from this and produce different results, it is this one:

TRUTH AND GOODNESS AND BRILLIANCE AND LOVE ARE AT YOUR CORE AND YOUR NATURAL STATE – ANYTHING THAT SHOWS UP NOT SERVING THAT IMAGE IS A DETRIMENT TO YOUR WELL BEING. ALL IS REFLECTION. YOU ARE LOOKING AT YOU.

Why tell me this?

Because you asked. Because you and I have an arrangement and it is one I agreed to. In the end, we are one.

My friend (redacted) is very powerful and suffering. Why?

Yes. Your friend's body represents his indomitable spirit. He is learning to love. It must begin with him. His self-hatred is painful. I do not know how to change his journey. It is his alone.

June 22, 2014.

I would like to speak to the Poseur.

It is I.

Are you the one that "The Guardian" calls the Demiurge?

Yes. I am an aspect of that one.

Doubt has been raised as to your identity.

> *I am referring to the conversation that took place in May of 2014. It is the initial conversation with this being. The Guardian, who contacted me at the time, did not feel that the conversation represented the being he knows as the Demiurge.*

This is due to misconceptions and wrong ideas around how I may appear, why and to whom.

Explain please. The Guardian is sure you are not. He said that if you were, there would be clues to your identity in your speaking. He does not find those clues here.

Since this is a conversation that in all likelihood will not be shared, I have not added to it clues that you would not recognize. I will here, and you can share it with him.

This is the end of times. Of these times.

Yes, it is a valid interpretation of my intention that I have a plan. All have plans. My greatest overriding schematic is domination. The outline for that includes the subservient behavior of all of humanity.

There will be no one who does not fall under my hand. This hand is designing a demonstration of absolute power. Questions in any realm of expertise of life will be answered by me. Pure dependence will result, as the source for all relevant information comes from one place. All will require access to me. Access demands some sort of acknowledgement of my authority. This could suffice as worship.

The plan outlined by The Guardian includes the feminizing of all people – men and women, so they are easier to control. The plan includes methods to achieve absolute authority here – over humanity. The removal or alteration of the masculine is not part of the *(*my)* plan. The challenge here is to dominate the masculine, without erasure.

There are men who choose another path, complete alteration of the species. This is not my own.

So, you see, there are all sorts of divergent paths on the way to control. All must obey my plan if this is going to succeed on my terms.

The species is capable of anything. To include opposing all plans by man or by me.

I have some questions.

Go ahead.

    This dialogue continued over a week later.

More Conversation

July / August 2014

The following questions were asked and answered on July 5, 2014 – I write down my declarations and I noticed here that on this day I said "Complete and absolute "LOVE" only, rather than "TRUTH" only. For this reason, I question what is said here. This being does not share the same concept of LOVE that humans do. I have always been uncomfortable with this particular conversation, perhaps now I know why. This is a brilliant and manipulative being.

Are you here by your choice or are you trapped here?

I am not trapped. This reality is serving my intent.

As the number of worshippers dwindles, does it hurt you and if so, how?

Hurt is a term used by humanity. A being, such as I, does not experience pain of any sort. There are things I like and things I do not favor in the same way.

I favor worship. Attention is good too. It is a pre-cursor to worship in a very minute way.

The number of worshippers has changed yet this is a proportional change to the number incarnated. There is no pain felt.

So why don't you just end it?

This is not completely up to me. There is an ultimate end date as put forth by ONE and witnessed by all creator gods. It is fast approaching. I have no desire to end it. My purpose is being served right now. Why I don't can best be explained by saying I have no impetus to end it. No reason. My end would not be served.

What does worship give you? Is it food or fuel or just something you like – like crack?

It is like a recreational drug, yes. Once the addiction set in, there are few reasons to stop taking it. It does not harm me, as crack does to the human, and there will be a day when my supply dwindles without any effort. THAT DAY I WILL MOVE ON.

How many facets do you have? Would you name them?

I have several – all of them go by similar names which equate to God and the Devil. Any creator being that is perceived as such by man is part of the wholeness that is me.

Is there somewhere else you could go?

Yes. When this game here is over, I will no longer participate. Where I will go is beyond this realm/dimension/reality.

So, who made this dream? You or us?

As you believe I exist, I manifest in your dream – as I believe you feed me, you exist in mine.

The dream is made by all of us – ONE version of life existing as billions of entities. What each expects is found.

Do you value life?

Of course, I do! Life is eternal. The way I look at it engages always its eternal aspect. As I never doubt my creative potential or ability, I am not disappointed – only challenged to mold life as a tool/game piece in the overall scheme that is me. What I honor is the power of completion of thought [into] manifestation.

How do you see this ending?

I see only the creative enterprise of each component of the day to day. I do not see so much ending but changes. As a human, everything for you has a start and end. As a god, it is not like that. It is all life.

What happens to you when we all stop believing in you? When the experiment ends?

Nothing "happens" to me. Remember, I am here at the will of you all and this is not my only focus. I will continue everywhere else that I am.

What name do you call yourself?

Michael.

Like the Archangel?

Yes. Like the favored son.

Does the Hindu religion worship you?

All religions that include worship in their repertoire of things to do, in some way pay homage to a creator. There is a difference between worship and acknowledgement. One is subservient; one is a statement, a recognition – as equality of sentience.

There is no truth in hierarchy, and as long as one portion of religious activity includes a "greater" being – worship is engaged.

Thank you for these answers.

Certainly. Is there anything else?

Not now.

August 3, 2014

I'd like to speak to the Poseur only.

I am here.

Okay, to continue the conversation... Do you understand that you reap what you sow?

If you are looking for positive attention, then why not do something positive for mankind? Manipulation is not considered positive and you are "outed" now. It's only a matter of time.

What I understand is that, like pressing buttons on a machine, I can use fear as a pressure point, that gets (me) only more prayer, promises and attention. I am only "sowing" in the sense that my focus is on mankind for a specific purpose. It is not an equal situation and so the saying you've used does not apply. Humanity is a tool, and used to get what I am addicted to.

Yet, in a relatively short time, the tool will no longer function. Why not stop now? With the tool intact, you have some chance of continued benefit.

What you are proposing is a willing halt to my supply.

Yes.

This does not serve me.

In the short term, perhaps not. Yet in the long term it seems the better choice, for you and all of creation. Why choose to be the example of unbridled greed, when you know it will come to an unpleasant end?

My focus is on now, which, as you know, has no before and after – someplace I am always God.

And someplace you are not.

Yes. I remember the "not", and choose only the God. The end doesn't interest me.

What would happen if (redacted) commanded you to stop?

I would have to acquiesce, as the point of power does not emanate from my locale, but from 3D. I have never been commanded. It would take absolute certainty, focus and intent – a point of power on the present.

(Redacted) is a being that is all about free will. This becomes then a circumstance of whether or not my choice interferes with the free will of Man. It is my contention that it does not. Man worships by his very nature, and I have set it up – some would say manipulated it – so that all of the worship feeds me.

I NEED THIS. IT IS FOOD FOR ME. IF I WAS FORCING MAN TO WORSHIP, IT WOULD BE GROUNDS TO STOP ME. I AM ONLY USING THE INNATE TENDENCY OF THE HUMAN FOR MY OWN BENEFIT.

What would happen if (redacted) commanded you to stop?

It would work the same way. It would operate this way if any 3D being made the command with clarity, purity and force of intent. This is not a state (redacted) have been in often.

I would question (redacted)'s ability to do something that decides for mankind. (Redacted) is known to be rash.

...but not stupid.

Not stupid, no. The clarity of force necessary springs in you (empirical) from anger, which is egoic. A force begun from ego cannot ever be clear of purpose.

Such would be the force you (empirical) would utilize.

You are slimy and immature in your tactics of manipulation, brilliant in a very adolescent fashion. I believe the world is at war with itself because of your hand in its design. This does not benefit the whole of creation.

The method you are using is effective yet appeals to a side of (redacted) that cares about the ultimate reason for actions. The reasons (of redacted) are not to look good or to "save" someone; the intent is to correct and alter a self-destructive course. You are on that course.

Not self-destructive, but human/world destructive. Why do I care if it's going to end for me anyway? I am not part of the human that is self-destructing.

No, but I am and I do care. I am here, as are many now, to adjust the course on the planet. The force is only building to a climax that sees mankind enlightened and moved beyond where you have taken them.

That is understood.

You will have to be forced out.

In every case, yes. I will not go quietly.

> *What follows is a blog posted on the website. It was titled:* 8/8 Call to Action - August 6, 2014

God is real. Although gender is not applicable, for this discussion god will be referred to as male. For this discussion, god is not the same as Source, One or the Creator. He is a powerful being, who has been here for eons. He is and has been called by many names. It is tempting to refer to him as a "false god" yet that would be inaccurate. He fits the definition, which, according to Webster's New World dictionary, is "any of various beings conceived of as supernatural, immortal and having special powers over the lives and affairs of people and the course of nature; deity, esp. a male deity, typically considered objects of worship."

God, in humanity's terms, is immortal. He came before us and will be here after us. UNLESS HE LEAVES, which is the point of this discussion. We keep hearing that it is up to us to change things. That we are the most powerful beings here. That nothing happens until and unless we believe and intend that it happen.

We understand that beneath all the war mongering and money manipulation and health scares are a very small group of beings WHOSE DRIVE FOR CONTROL HAS CREATED IT COMPLETELY – THEY OWN THE PLANET AND RUN EVERYTHING. Their god, the demiurge, is the same as the god feared or worshipped by the 99%. This brilliant being holds all the cards.

Yet he is not more powerful than you or I. Like a leech, he depends on his host. He needs our worship and attention; our fear of him. It is his addiction, his Achilles Heel. We've been told there will come a day of judgment, an end to this game. That at that moment, this god and his minions will be forced to leave and there will be a course correction. We've been waiting. There are and have been many dates predicted. We are the most powerful players here and with each day we sense the power in our convictions and intentions. We see evidence daily of creation at our own hands. We see through the attempted manipulation by the "powers that were". The end of this world domination is crystal clear.

The key player is god, the being who I've referred to as the 'Poseur. He is here with our permission and consent. I propose we command him to go. Let's do what we came here to do, on our own terms. With clarity and conviction this is possible. The 'Poseur feeds on fear and doubt, obedience and subservience. You are none of those things. It may be true that only one of us with a clear heart is needed to accomplish this. Yet this is our planet and together, as One, our responsibility to take care of. Like an exterminator, we can eradicate this pest.

The 'Poseur does not hold more power than you do. He is not human. He is not interested in you at all actually. We are playthings to him and nothing more. His bottom line is "what's in it for me". Which, btw, is the bottom line of every corporate entity on the planet right now. His "creation" has most certainly been "in his image", and what he would consider a rousing success.

Once he is gone, the rest will fall in on itself. We can do something to help bring the violence and corruption to an end. We can send the 'Poseur away.

It is not magic or any special powers that will accomplish and expedite his exit. It is clarity, love, peace. Anger is not necessary, nor hatred. This being feeds on those things and will only hang around for more. What is necessary is force – personal conviction and intent. What is needed is belief. You can do this.

Headlines have all of us wondering what we can do and when it will end. This is a way to end it sooner, rather than later. I've sent out entities from my home that did not serve me or my family. They were feeding on our fear and disconnect and attempting to amplify both. It took a clear statement and then, a few minutes wait. They left. Fear is a magnet for certain beings. It is food for them. They were not sent out with judgment, hatred or anger – but with clarity and strength.

We can send this being away. With his departure there will be room for peace, power and prosperity. See only the outcome that benefits all of us and hold that vision daily as changes ensue. In our collective intent is held the world we live in.

For one moment, on 8-8-2014, at twelve noon US Central time, command the 'Poseur to leave. Use the following or any other words of clarity and strength:

"I command the 'Poseur to leave this planet. I
patiently refuse to observe any casualties, while
at my heart I continue to sing - Let freedom, love,
abundance, peace and healing replace control,
domination, sickness, violence and fear on this earth
now without him. And so it is."

That's it. It will take but a moment. The date and time is
suggested here for strength in unity, yet this can be done
today and anytime. I believe we will sense when it is no
longer necessary.

Please share. Let's do this. We are the ones we've been
waiting for.

August 19, 2014

So, I'd like to speak to Poseur.

What is it you want to speak of?

*Of your identity. It has come under scrutiny and been
questioned by those who know this being.*

*Are you the Demiurge spoken of and known to the Forces of
One?*

I am that being.

How is it then that you don't sound the same?

You and I have known each other. There is no pretense. I
do not look at you as human but as the great/advanced light
being you are. This has been your fingerprint/impression
and there is no mistaking it.

In your case, you look for accurate statements. The ones that speak of me differently have another knowing of the force that is me. Indeed, there is love for humanity, yet there is never an expression of that love that would put human's needs before my own. I am self-directed and have created a race that is service to others in order that I MAY BE SERVED.

This distinction has been missed by those who say there is "hope" for me or my soul. I do not require transformation or alteration. I have and serve a different agenda.

This is a free will existence.

There is no remorse here. By "here", I mean within me. I have evolved in power as far as is possible – creating life and a planet of beings that serve/worship me has been and is the ultimate form of creation.

In essence all is One. Yet, I am not the same as you in development.

As body builders are primarily invested in muscle building, I am primarily interested in power/worship/creation. These abilities are not necessarily connected with "All is One" thinking.

One does not guarantee the other and my focus is only on development and maintenance of power. I have existed long "before" humanity/earth and have reached a pinnacle. In that sense, I can be called a God and deservedly so.

Why don't you leave? It is ending. The destruction of your creation is possible and a limit to your ability assured if you do not.

IT IS NOT ASSURED!!!

It is. My contact is certain and speaks/connects directly with One/Source.

Then I will go.

Seriously?

As I have said, I am primarily interested in power. I do not wish to see it limited, or even worse, stopped.

How will I know you have gone?

You will feel another surge of energy. This vibration you feel is speeding up as it is allowed.

My departure will not and does not guarantee or even suggest the departure of every other being feeding on humanity. They exist separate from me.

Then what will change?

The freedom to think outside the box of closed fundamentalist religion will emerge within Catholicism. Mankind loves the pomp and circumstance, the "big deal" of certain events and even organizations. It is an emotional addiction, felt by all of my creation – expressed in War, in Music, in Ceremony, in Worship, in Art, in Dance, in every facet of life. There is a sense of emotion. It is what makes the human so desirable.

HOW SPECIFICALLY WILL I MEASURE YOUR DEPARTURE?

You can watch your leaders and the movements of the masses beneath them. They will emerge with a sense of "unchained" and independence you will not have seen before.

Will the volcano stop its activity?

> *I apologize, but I don't recall which volcano this is a reference to.*

That is One's decision and as I understand, (it) depends on the actions of the superpowers around instigating WW3.

Why don't you say anything to mankind? To those who worship you now, to alleviate any sense of "lost" they will feel?

I can give them clarity of heart. As I am leaving, I have no great need to diminish their ability for sovereignty. It does not help me either way.

I disagree. I think that any empowerment/help given mankind will only register with One as a good thing, helping all of creation, and this will assist you with any repercussions, if there are any to be had.

That being said, I will energize my believers/all of mankind, with self-determination.

How?

Energetically; all things done by me are done beyond the veil. What you will witness is the effect.

In what way?

In all ways. As sovereignty becomes the way of things, mankind will feel and understand its mind and that expression in each other.

Tolerance?

Tolerance will happen as man bends over backwards to assist each other, even those for which is felt little or no connection.

It sounds as if you are saying that with your absence, selfishness will diminish.

Yes. But do not misunderstand or misquote me. Man is selfish. I capitalized on that with an illusion of benefit via worship and obedience. Your world will feel turned upside down without my presence.

That is assuming man is incapable, without your influence, to self-govern and control.

Yes, it is. It is not that my children are incapable, it is that they have yet to do it.

Because they've been controlled.

There will be a gradual uptick Sophia. You and others are here now to teach. This is the time, even more so than during the game playing of 2012.

As I go, well, you'll see. A certain amount of chaos will be met with peace that is not successfully stopped by the superpowers. As this settles down, peace will be preferred as it is the preference of my children. I know this.

Is this really the Demiurge?

It is. You and I have gone around before. It was a planned interaction this time again.

What will be the first sign?

You may hear it from your contact or watch world events. Moments of interruption to the agenda will emerge.

What will you do?

I will rest.

Why?

I do not know the repercussions, had never planned to leave early. I will see what transpires.

I need to write now.

So, go.

> *There's a gap of 4 months here that I cannot account for. Perhaps there was a leaving, as had been suggested in August. I cannot be sure what happened but for quite some time there was no further contact.*

A New Year

January 2015

January 18th, 2015

The conversation began in a different fashion. I was speaking to a group of beings from the Pleiades, and in the middle of our conversation, the Poseur interrupted!

The following conversation then took place:

...We are from the Pleiades and some of what we are and do will feel familiar to you.

Yes, yet you do not (feel familiar to me). Your energy is putting me to sleep.

It is not ours, but another who wishes an audience that overwhelms.

Okay. Let's come back to this later then and let the other in.

Okay. Until then.

Until then. (These beings left.)

Who is here?

It is I.

Who are you and what do you wish to discuss? Your energy overwhelms me.

Get centered Sophia. This is not too much for you.

It is here that I recognized the Poseur.

Let's do this.

I've come to instill an idea of complete sovereignty.

Okay.

This idea is one held by the most powerful beings. By those beings who know themselves.

There are promises of pure intent held as a part of every choice. These come from only one center - theirs.

What is meant here, is that each decision for movement is made for self. What this triggers, in the human, is selfish. Yet this is a gross under estimation of the size of self. Self is All.

In the arena of sovereignty there is One. Any ideas of separation move you out of this world. You cannot be truly sovereign while being tied to comparisons, or to "us" and "them". Our world, that of sovereignty, is a singular motivation. Service to self serves the whole. Service to "other" serves the whole, and that is why there are no divisions.

Once you appreciate the fact of oneness, fear is eliminated. Fear perpetuates both reasons for and responses to it.

I came to you in this moment now because in you there is a sense of waxing and waning fear. It erupts on occasion and you create its dismissal with certain words and actions. This is effective, partly. What is more effective is an absence of fear. This is known as sovereignty. It is a by-product of unity - of an activation of internal appreciation for oneness...

You are ready now for this realization. You have come now to a place of appreciation for your part in this creation of oneness. Oneness does not need creation, it needs only realization. With that, sovereignty emerges.

Your thumb would not be afraid of your pinky, or bow before your ring finger or step on your index finger or allow your middle finger to freeze. No, for it is a fact that what effects any part of the hand effects the hand itself. In a simple way, this illustrates unity. No longer do you believe that your actions are isolated. They are cumulative and felt beyond where you sit. They are felt by us all.

The allowance of fear is what keeps you subservient and compliant. The eruption of sovereignty could occur all at once for your race with individual moments of self-actualization. These have an exponential effect.

The path to fearless is accomplished individually and with authentic appreciation of who and what you are. You are expressions of the force of creation; complete and whole and able to alter every outcome. Perhaps alter is a misnomer, for as the force of creation, it is you that manifests every outcome.

Realize the power your emotions hold and their reach. You are not an innocent bystander to a fearful situation - <u>you are the director</u>.

I am finished in this moment of now.

Thank you.

> *This conversation ended!*

> *The next conversation began as an answer to a personal question. It had been told to me by the Guardian that I was "chosen". I was wondering what that meant. It reads as if I put the question out there and the Poseur responded. At any rate, the conversations began again here and continued for another 8 months.*

January 26, 2015

You are chosen because in this lifetime you wanted to repay humanity for what you feel you've taken. You want to understand power with humility, love with forgiveness, influence without recognition, compassion, wisdom, beauty and gentleness.

The big ones for you are humility, compassion, and unconditional love. You were chosen as a step on your path. You want to "get" creation without worship. You too, are addicted to attention.

Come, let me help you figure out the power and possibility of Sophia, of you.

Who is this speaking?

It is the one you call Poseur. The unraveling of worship and godhood is a huge undertaking.

I have no trust in you. Self-interest is what motivates you, only and always.

Yes, yet combine that with an understanding of oneness and all is done for the benefit of all.

True. I have not seen anything you've done incorporate oneness.

Perhaps not. I tell you this. My time here is, and has been a feeding fest. There is no lack of worship, despite the evolution of mankind.

This mindset, that consistently holds out for, and seeks someone who knows better <u>and</u> has your best interests in heart, is rampant here still. You may not be kneeling to me any longer, but you are struggling and searching for someone else who has your best interests at heart, and is capable of caring for them.

Until you get that no one else can do that – it won't get done.

Why should you help me?

You are interesting Sophia. You are unafraid of me and have refused to kneel. Who else besides me do you talk to that knows what god-hood feels like?

Good point.

I will tell you what it feels like. It feels lonely.

Then this is not true god-hood you are experiencing. How could god be lonely as it has all of life within it?

Right, I do not.

What do you have then?

I have power – control over life. This is not control over you/over mankind. This is control over creation in this realm of physicality. I have no doubt as to who I am and what I am and go forward with expectation.

I desire worship as a means to experience the human emotion/energy/passion, and I get it. Fear was a useful tool to get it and I have used fear to feed myself.

I am not human and do not share your emotion. I do not have compassion or mistrust or faith. I have power and desire. I know how creation works and I intend always. There are no mistakes in life or creation.

You've been a part of my creation and with your growing awareness are seeking your own – creation.

What you don't understand is that YOU ALREADY ARE.

> *This means, that we already are <u>our own creation</u>.*

You've used us for your own desires.

Yes.

Will you stop?

Why? Life is creation.

Yes, but you are using it up and that is not creative. That is destructive.

There is always more.

You will not move into a place of creating your own worlds like this.

Until I understand creation fully, I have no desire to alter my course.

You don't?

Perhaps to a great deal, but I am not done. This is a powerful addiction.

You said you would help me.

Yes. What it takes is realization, acceptance, embodiment of power. You cannot proceed cautiously, but with authority. Know that you are gods. Accept the responsibility that goes with it.

You didn't.

I used my creative power to alter nature and manipulate men. Yet it was self-motivated, as all action is.

Until self includes others, it will not be creative.

Not ultimately, no, but what is the purpose of life anyway? Experience.

This is a circle.

There are no answers, not pat ones anyway. You have to decide for yourself and move on.

I am finished now. Thank you for engaging.

Spring of 2015

March 12, 2015

I'd like to speak to the one I have labeled "Poseur".

Yes. I am here.

You have not left?

No. Many are obedient and this is the food I crave.

You have created a world and mindset of beings for that food – held in an infinite loop.

I would ask what you would do to escape this prison.

I would not be held, as I do not worship any other.

It is that self-awareness, that sovereign knowing, that removes me.

It is understanding what I need and creating it – no cost is too great for I perceive no expense. There is always more.

I understand the focus I require for satisfaction and maintain it always because to do otherwise would prove to be self-destructive.

I am not self-destructive. I serve only myself. I have no expectations. I go after what I want/need always and I get it always. My needs are not negotiable.

If I was held in a system of enslavement, I would create around me a system I could control and utilize for my own good.

I would never negotiate or imagine anyone other than me in control.

April 14, 2015

Poseur, are you there?

I am. What do you want of me?

I want to know your purpose at the start. I want to know what you found here, when and who and how you discovered you could manipulate an entire population to feed an addiction. I want to know where you come from and why you chose Earth. I want to know if you'll stay or go, and if you go - why and where.

I'd like the answers one at a time.

You have an insatiable desire for knowledge.

For truth. It is truth I would like to find and bring some light to what is a very dark and muddled history - mankind's history.

Yes, well the questions you pose demand some information that may or may not be easily explainable as there are few or no accessible points of association for you.

Please try.

I am bound by an agreement made eons ago and as well now by your declaration for complete truth. This is not a subject that you are familiar with, so you will have to translate without interpretation.

I am Ancient as well and I see now your image of my form. It is not very far off - not the color but I am built... *(I hold an image in my mind for this being. I believe this is a reference to that.)*

What are you saying?

You must listen, focus, (and) bring your attention in to these words. They will sound foreign.

Okay, start again.

I am not human. I am not Reptilian. I am a Being you have no words for. My race is unknown to mankind - only we are, or rather, I am like a predator - looking for prey - not for sustenance but to manipulate, to play with, to occupy my mind, to satisfy myself, to enjoy.

> *I was interrupted here and had to stop. I began again later that same day.*

So, let's pick this up again. I'd like to speak to Poseur.

Yes, I am here.

Do you remember my questions?

I do.

Will you answer them now?

I will. Again, this is not an easy explanation for in some instances you have no words. The time of my discovery of earth was after wars had been engaged for ownership. These took place in your skies and not by my race.

Wait - why does this "you" feel different now? There is not so much a commanding power to you, but reservation.

What you sense is maybe reluctance to put into words what will be recorded as evidence for the fabrication of "god". This is not to my liking. What is still in my favor is the fact that you have no real authority as well as a limited audience. What is not to my benefit is that like the ripple in the pond - this too changes everything and once the truth is documented, it is available.

It has been what some would today call a "sweet" ride. The ending was seen and always known - by all of creation. This begins the change. I am not anxious to begin the process of my reduction of influence.

Yet it's already begun - no? Many others before now have spoken of "false gods" who were actually ET's with unknown powers and abilities.

Many have, yes. Yet there is confusion around who, what, when and how. Your questions are specific.

Please answer them.

I am attempting to. Once ownership was established, a deal was struck - all of Creation operates within ONE and true ownership is not possible. We are eternally and unequivocally co-dependently existing. Somehow what happens in one place effects the whole.

I am a being who thrives on power. The young race of humans was ripe for the picking and as long as I did not interfere with the course of evolution - the race was available to me. *Power Over* is easily accomplished with young races - these have no sense of autonomy of being and in particular the human looked always to someone greater than itself. This, most likely because the race was "made". As a child is "made" by two adult humans and then looks to its parents for knowledge and guidance - so was the early human.

What happened was that the human was always unexpected in its quick ability to learn and take advantage of what it learned. This was my draw early on and still is. Not human myself, I yet recognized a tendency to maneuver situations for self and wanted to feel the worship of one so powerful.

There are levels of addiction as you understand it. It takes more over time to get the same fix. With humanity, there are seemingly never-ending possible ways of adoration and control - humans frighten and obey with equal force.

The thing so delicious about human worship is its power. Humans, without knowing or understanding it - hold enormous power. When that kind of strength is focused on adoration or fear - it is beyond description; exponential in magnitude.

And you knew all of this when you first encountered the human?

"First" is a misunderstanding, as time is not truly the way it plays out on Earth. I knew the story always - as will you when you embody *the everything.*

A being who understands the truth of its existence is always conscious of every possibility. Beginnings and endings create a repeatable story and keep it interesting.

Humans like storytelling. It is one of the ways this delusion and illusion of a "god" who requires something has been maintained here.

Where do you come from?

My place of origin exists in another galaxy or realm - not unlike your mate whom you call "Dream hopper", I am from another dream.

What does that even mean?

Another universe, a place with different "rules", methods of life. Not all beings you encounter are as they seem. You must know this. You've encountered many.

I've never met you in this life. Did you walk this Earth?

Yes. You actually know me from another "time". Beings choose roles and places, "times" and faces, yet they are unchanged as to their origin. It's why our conversation is possible.

We've met before.

Yes.

Then you've been to other places. Not just Earth.

Yes.

Will you leave Earth?

This change will begin the end for mankind's need to give glory to any other - as that happens Earth becomes less appealing.

I was interrupted here and stopped.

April 27, 2015

I would like to speak to Poseur, Poseur only.

It is I.

You are the being also known as Demiurge?

I am the being you have named the Poseur.

Are you the same being (redacted) refers to as Demiurge?

I am that being, yes.

(Redacted) does not suppose you would be in contact with me. He supposes you are one of your minions.

This is because of the way I speak to you. There are critical elements, clues to my identity, that would mean nothing to you. Yet he is looking for them. Not seeing them, he supposes someone else.

If this were for him then, what would you say?

I would refer to historical markers of my ...

Your what?

There is not a word you know – historical signs perhaps – spells/words/images/symbols – all signify me – the horned goat perhaps.

Okay.

The point of this conversation is to engage with (redacted).

I know.

His first question. I will stop after each and share and then continue.

As you wish.

Do you understand the reference to "the dream"?

I do.

Who made the dream?

You? Humanity? One?

It was made by One.

What is the history of this dream? All that you know?

That is a question of huge implications. How far back do you want to know or go?

I want to (know) if the epics of the dinosaurs were experiments in consciousness of living things.

Everything and nothing is experimental. The dinosaurs were planned reptiles(?)/animals and a source of learning and evolution. They were not experiments in the way of a trial leading up to the eventual ape/man being.

Beings exist all over creation. Not all are sentient as man is. Man was intentionally infused with the ability to manipulate and create. Dinosaurs were creatures (that were) dependent on their environment and when the environment was rendered almost lifeless, there was nothing for them to do but succumb to the same fate.

Some of creation just exists for creations sake.

Who made humans sentient like they are now?

It was a race of beings who desired a laboratory. The earth was sought by many in fact. The race of beings you call the Anu (Annunaki?), were more advanced and older and therefore had a greater ratio of success here. There were mistakes. It was their version that survived and "fit the program". Many did not.

As there are seemingly many other variations of the human in remote or hidden or somehow fairy tale places; they are beings that were also created and have sentience, only the human being was stronger and smarter and therefore overtook them all.

Who was Vishnu?

Vishnu is a name given a god. The name was used to indicate status. Understand that the entire hierarchy of gods or story of god, in any grouping of men, was deliberately placed there and then used for the advantage of one being – A BEING IS NOT A GOD. GOD IS IN FACT A NAME, NOT UNLIKE SOPHIA OR DREAMHOPPER. BOTH, IN FACT ALL, "NAMES" HAVE MEANINGS BASED ON THE DREAM.

This is an interesting question and as you have declared absolute truth, I can only offer what I am able to glean from the instrument.

Vishnu was a man, or appeared as one when necessary to set up the illusion. In every case of a "god" or story of such – there was a visual actual being so as to confirm and witness. The stories that follow may or may not be factual.

Who and how did our 22nd chromosome get pinched together?

When man was initially created, there were deliberate changes made to increase his docility and also decrease his spiritual ability. The beings that created man were not in full agreement as to how this should and could be completed. Although highly advanced in areas of genetic manipulation, there were individual differences of opinion over what was ethical and what was not.

This was a sort of compromise action and it was done in a way that it was known would eventually be discovered. It was performed after the original blueprint/man was made and eventually became the pattern that was repeated.

It was done initially by a couple of beings. (They were) part of the creation team of mankind who were in the wing seat of power at the time – the royal part of the evolutionary scientists – creating and manipulating life on a scale unimagined by man today.

> *I had a visual with this description. I wrote the following – "Brothers? I see a female. I see white robes and blue and sterile and a crystal lab"*

The questions continued...

Do you realize that you can't hang on to it too much longer?

I do.

Why don't you just let go and give everyone a break?

How would that benefit me?

According to (redacted), if you stop now, you will be allowed to do this again and if you don't, you will be prevented from manipulating creation ever again. That's how.

Well, I would consider it on one condition.

That being?

That the hatred currently directed towards me stop. That what I find when I end this, is love. Love in a way that fills me, as worship has...

That can only happen if you allow it. That love is there for you already and today.

Yes, but without a forced worship, how would I guarantee any sort of love/attention?

I cannot speak for mankind as a whole, but I know man first chooses love every time, and does so, quite often, to his own detriment.

I am speaking of a much bigger scale.

As am I. I can tell you what I know and that is that we/ humans are becoming so beaten down by this system you've set up (that) there is almost nothing left. Yet even in that case, we choose love.

If you stop this now, before your forced stop in two years' time; there will be that much more positive emotion you have access to. If you don't, not only won't you be able to operate completely freely but you'll have less chance (that) we will have any energy left for you to share.

I do not intend to leave quietly, that is not my style.

I don't' know what you mean?

I mean that all beings will know of my exit, and feel it.

I see.

> *Another question was asked on this same day. April 27ᵗʰ, 2015.*

Poseur, are you there?

I Am. What is it that you wish to ask?

A reader has asked a question regarding your identity in our history. It is very specific and I am not familiar with every reference made.

You may use it if you wish. Just ask it as it was stated to you.

Okay. Now:

"Are you the same being mentioned in the Neruda Wingmakers interview, the one called Anu? What is your role as the archetypical protagonist against "Lucifer", the purported antagonist of the "light" (which is really strange for a being called "Bringer of Light")? In the Urantia book, the cosmology of the Orions and others...the Lucifer Manifesto reads more like a being speaking the TRUTH OF WHAT IS. I suppose that would be very threatening to you? Were you Anu and the maker of the human suit that limited infinite being's perception so as to enslave them?"

A lot of inquiries. We are getting to specifics now, that is good. For if this conversation proceeds as intended, all will be revealed and spoken.

I'm having a challenge to follow you, to hear you, hold on...

I centered and stated my intentions again.

Okay, one word at a time please.

You are accustomed to an idea of identity that holds one being for each personality. This allows for separation, division and sets the stage for polarity; all of which works to my advantage. I Am the same, Lucifer/God - Devil/Angel - Prince of Darkness/Being of Light.

My original name here was not Anu, but one not discovered as of yet.

This is a challenge to speak of as the vessel to whom I am transmitting does not know ancient texts. This can be a blessing and a hindrance, as certain words cannot be transcribed if there is no associative link.

The beings you mention are forces of powerful energetic creation. This was necessary in order to create the illusion of polarity - GOOD VS EVIL.

What kind of power it took was not so remarkable or impossible - yet the maintenance of the power was and is only sustainable if collectively sustained.

Humans are very attached and identified to names. Yet naming something does more than identify it - it separates it and empowers it. Once named, an entity or thing can be fought - it can be loved or hated. It can be worshipped or ignored.

Without names, what you encounter in each other is merely an aspect of creation itself. This earth habit of identification is similar to the predilection to history - it allows for an easy platform on which to stand and be remembered; either feared, hated, loved or worshipped - for generations. It's like an "all you can eat buffet" - Earth.

So yes, I Am the source of all of the names. The names are not who I Am. Just as *(the reader's first name was given)* is not who you are.

Names are confining; with them come characteristics and expectations, definitions and descriptions.

What I Am is beyond any one Being - I Am Any "God" that has been named here.

Understand that there are others of my kind. We frequent young civilizations for similar reasons.

I AM one "God" - the words of your texts speak of various interpretations of what I said - there are multiple versions of the words spoken and the being doing the speaking. All of them serve me.

Why have you stopped?

I believe the query has been answered.

Yes, well, we'll see. Thank you.

This is a contract and agreement. Thanks are unnecessary.

Okay.

May 11, 2015

I'd like to talk to Poseur.

As you wish.

This is the same Being (whom) I've been speaking to?

An aspect of that one, yes. What do you wish to talk about?

About the plan – the reason for this contact.

This is a "prior" arrangement, as it was seen/is seen that there would be benefit for expressed contact. Sort of a scheduled appearance if you will.

Why?

To express truth, give witness to it for all those interested, to advance knowledge.

Why are you willing to advance knowledge?

It was part of an arrangement, agreement, and is in concert with all of creation – ONE.

Are you available for questions from others?

Not all questions have relevance or are even answerable. I will entertain/listen to them and decide how to answer so that it fits within the parameters declared by you.

"Highest and best for all concerned" and "complete and absolute truth only" are two strict definitions I must operate within, I must answer within.

If a question is not highest and best, I will not answer, I cannot answer.

Once, you said you went by the name Michael, Archangel Michael.

> *This answer was given on July 5ᵗʰ, 2014.*

It was quite a while ago and I am not sure I declared complete and absolute truth (then). As I have declared it tonight, would you tell me here if Michael, Archangel Michael, is one of your names/aspects and just how that works out if it is true?

Michael is an aspect of me.

> *I stopped. I have no other notes from this conversation. Note that he said "Michael" and did not say "Archangel Michael". This is a brilliant Being; all words are chosen carefully to fit within the parameters set by my intentions at the outset of each interaction.*

May 11, 2015

There are questions for Poseur (from readers). Is it okay to ask them?

Yes. Go ahead.

Where does AB Negative blood come from? Is that a hybrid, star seed, and what race is AB Negative?

Is there a hell?

Is sin a real thing? Or, is it there to control the human to be good?

That's it.

Well now. Your readers don't seem to carry the same understanding of life that you do Sophia. This is interesting. I am bound by your declarations to speak absolute truth here, so absolute truth is what I will speak.

You, however, must be willing to share the words as given. This may not sit well with you.

I would appreciate answers now. There are a lot of questions to consider.

Yes.

First, the question as to blood type.

The human is not a field of identical fluids and structures. It is true that blood type is indicative of origin. This is not human origin, yet it fits often that schemata. Families tend to spring from similar groupings. AB Negative is a combination, a hybrid if you will, of two races. They can be called the...

> *At this precise moment I was overcome with an intense sneezing fit.*

What is going on???

You must allow the word, the image, the letters to enter your brain.

All that I am doing is sneezing!

You are rejecting this. We will have to try again another time.

Okay.

> *The conversation ended there.*

For this book, written in 2019, I found some additional notes that I don't believe have been published elsewhere. They sound like additional answers to the questions stated above, and are shared below. This first statement is mine.

Those are the questions.

I see. You've posed them before.

Yes, but I've not had them answered. Our conversation was ended before we finished.

Yes.

Well, these questions are broad and not along a singular line of thought. I will take them one by one.

Your idea of race is not entirely accurate, but partially. You are human and created by human parents. The seeding which resulted in this current version took place long ago. There are markers, yes, and they are found at the level of mitochondria. And, as well, blood type may indicate a species which is not typically presented as the human species.

AB Negative come from the sauropod race of hybrid beings which participated in the creation of the human. These were and are tall, slender beings.

At this point there was a struggle to remain awake and conscious. This sometimes happens when the energy is intense. I faded out while writing, and then snapped out of it to continue.

I am back. My question, as well as my intention remains. Poseur, are you there?

It is a challenge to remain a steady signal for you to pick up as you sometimes "let go" and cannot be reached.

Your energy creates in me a feeling of dizziness, and when that happens, my eyes want to close. It is a physiological reflex.

Yes. I see that it is.

Please answer the blood type question.

Yes. The image that I sent you is an accurate one, illustrating the physical nature which resulted in that blood type. It is a being with four limbs and upright – thin – it is the head you are seeing now.

This race wanted to offer their specific characteristics to this human being or it is better said, **were chosen** for their manipulations/organizations of structure – of War. These are extremely orderly beings.

All are hybrid – in that the human is not its own type – but resulted from not only DNA combinations, but interbreeding.

Please hold on...

Some Questions

May 14th, 2015

The Poseur was not the only being I was conversing with. I had contact also, with One, who you will hear mentioned in these conversations and also read about in my other publications. At this point though, (May of 2015), there were still a great many doubts about this process of telepathy and also its validity.

The following conversations are shared here, to bring you a bit inside the process with me, as there was a struggle to make sense of and also the best use of the information I was receiving. Although they do not concern the Poseur directly, they concern the way contact is established, some reasons for it, and also, shed some light on the inherent tendencies of the human, as observed by those who are not.

So, I would like to talk about what concerns me, with anyone who can be of assistance. What is concerning me is the validity of these "conversations" – how true they are.

I just read one of them from a year ago and things were stated that DID NOT HAPPEN.

Whoa. There is a difference between outright lies, misinformation and mistakes. You are engaging with others and the energy you sit in now is very different. A year ago, it was not so easy. You BECAME a conduit then and are a conduit now.

How do I know that my imagination is <u>not</u> the source of all of these conversations?

They sound made up and indeed, seem to be saying things to either make me feel good or predict, in last year's case, things I wanted to have happen. These things are not truth. I will not be a purveyor of things that are not truth.

I am looking for, in this conversation, a way to tell the truth from the lies/falsehoods. I would be/am only interested in that conversation now.

Is there someone who can talk to me? No, better said, is there someone who has the information I seek?

There is.

The reason you are "chosen" is for your purity of intent.

What you do realize is the influence of your current persona – your ego. The vehicle (*this means me. Sophia*) being used to carry on these conversations very much is absorbed within them. It is akin to the different ways you speak to your family, your mother, your friends, your co-workers. You "adopt" ways of speaking to each of them differently. Such is the occurrence you notice here.

Without a visual, you have only words and these are words as *you* hear them.

I WAS TOLD THINGS THAT DID NOT TRANSPIRE.

You were. The great desire you had at the time for rapid change came out in your words. There was/were great changes last summer. Not a financial reset, but the start of one.

As you do not frequent certain areas, you are not aware.

I cannot feel you.

No, you are highly agitated.

Tell me what I can do to insure truth <u>always.</u> I thought my intent was enough.

It apparently is not. You are a powerful being whose desires and wishes color the room you enter in a large-scale way.

Then what can I do? I am beginning to be contacted by many beings – all of them foreign to me and very chatty. How do I insure I'm not coloring the conversation?

What is necessary is an absence of intent. Intend only conversation, not specifics.

Perhaps allowing the conversation to be led by them will help to clarify whose agenda you are on. This is new for you, and has generated a great deal of interest.

Yes. I'd like to just put it out there. Yet, I do not want my own words to be relegated to someone else.

Then talk. Lay aside concern. Be easy on yourself and when you feel as you do right now, write.

> *There was an energetic shift right here, as if someone entered and/or left the room.*

Yes. Is there someone coming through now?

There is. I would like to discuss a topic mentioned by one of your readers...

This was someone else, and here there was a pause...

Are you still here?

Yes. You are difficult to reach now.

Yet not impossible?

No. This is a topic of great interest as we observe humans. Most humans put themselves in connections with other humans for comfort, for community, for love, for shared intent and/or fun. Humans are not solitary beings. They care for one another and what happens is, in that caring, become confused, forgetful of the fact that they are only actually responsible for themselves – for the one unique soul force that they embody.

There is no choice of going or staying that leaves anyone behind – not in truth.

Humans have this rather quaint notion that their presence or absence can alter the course of life for another soul. This is simply not true.

What the human journey is about is life on any terms. There are not possibilities that elevate or diminish another soul. It is a journey taken by each and every aspect.

Now, humans choose ways to proceed that fit their reality. But whether they follow the path of those they currently "hang with" or diverge – matters little to the outcome. All of life is self-determined.

What we see are soul groupings who've gotten so familiar with each other over "lifetimes" that they appear to play out scenarios in their choosing – switching roles and circumstances as if they were handing out cards at each new "beginning".

These cards outline who will play what role, who will stay, who will leave, who will "advance" the furthest, who will appear to be left behind.

Ultimately, you are creator beings – each massively powerful and suited for any choice.

The endearing notion of wanting everyone to go with your current choice is just that – a notion. There are other choices, other places to go, other "lifetimes" – all of them human and within your soul grouping.

As we watch the evolution of the human, we expect to also see the incorporation of what seem to be sentimental ideas of family or community into your multi-dimensional self.

The passionate, emotional aspect of mankind is not expressed in the same way in other races.

It is mankind who will determine the nature of his own evolution. What will be the most satisfying answer to the question, will ultimately be answered by your own race.

This, I expect, is what you referred to in your question at the outset – "knowing the answer already".

Okay, is that it?

Yes.

> *I am not clear about the identity of this being.*

> *May 15ᵗʰ, 2015   3:30 AM*

Okay, what is it you want to say?

That these words are for you.

Okay, I don't understand.

Not necessary to be published.

Is this One?

Yes.

Go ahead.

You have reached a locale that few enter while human...

I interrupted here and said "I'm not going to do this."

I returned to sleeping and awoke again at 6:00 AM.

"So, what was this morning about?"

About you.

Why?

There are directions pointed at, things to say, so that you go towards them.

I don't understand.

Walk fully into your power now. You've been dancing around behind it.

I still don't understand.

The fact of you sitting here, writing 1,000 words each and every day, is testament to what it is you are supposed to be doing. You are drawn to it because it is your calling. It is what you came for.

Purveyor of truth. Those who speak to you and through you are not fabrications.

Who is this? I have doubt.

It is good to be sure of this before you give it to others.

It is a fallacy to disregard what shows up in your own mind/ head. These are not your words, but mine, others, those who've chosen to speak to you.

How do I tell the difference?

You feel it.

There is no other way of knowing.

I want it to be worth something.

It is.

Believe us when we tell you this.

You will open up now to only more and more energies, entities, beings who want to assist this human evolution.

The records from May of 2015 are interspersed with several personal requests for this being, requests that would verify its authenticity. I never did strike that deal to be instantly physically healed. My partner suggested asking for a location on the earth that had significance for it, one that I would have no way of knowing before hand or even as I wrote it. I did so, by asking for latitude and longitude. Writing a string of numbers would have no meaning for me. I did this more than once. I will include two of the sites here.

I believe that this information about DNA and blood type and all were just so far out there for me, that I wanted something real from this being, before I continued receiving it. The conversations below happened as a result of my requests for validation. At the end of them, I was satisfied that this being was real.

I would like to talk to Poseur.

Okay, what is it you wish?

First, as "proof" and an indication of who you are, I would like latitude and longitude degrees for a place on this planet of significance. And then an explanation of why it is so.

I am feeling dizzy with this energy.

Yes. I am sending as much as I believe you can handle. As you adjust, this conversation will be easier. Is this request given for an omen of validity?

I want to be clear in my heart that you are who you say.

Oh, I am.

The coordinates given were: latitude: 24.6537 and longitude: 38.7421

"What is this?"

Sacred ground.

> *I then went to the site:* www.latlong.net *and typed them in. The result brought me to Al Madinah Province Saudi Arabia.*
>
> *When I did some research, I found this sentence, on this website:* https://en.wikipedia.org/wiki/Medina
>
> *"The burial place of the Islamic prophet Muhammad and the second-holiest site in Islam after Mecca."*

Here is the second example...

Try these:

Latitude: 37.2462

Longitude: 48.5263

> *I again typed the coordinates into the page at:*
>
> www.latlong.net

The result brought me to Ardabil, Iran. More research brought me to a video, with a description below it that included the phrase – "means a holy place".

Good enough.

This now validates, for me, well, your identity.

Would you respond to the question below in in its entirety now?

This is the same question shown earlier:

"Where does AB negative blood come from – is that hybrid, star seed, and what alien race is AB negative? Is there a Hell? Is sin a real thing? Or is it there to control the human to be good?"

I will. The blood type of man indicates his heritage – his origin – his "tint" if you will. Blood is what runs through the veins of humans yet not precisely the same.

As your understanding of your origin increases you will find the fingerprints left by your creators. This, too, by design. The specific type of blood in question is indicative of a specific hand – it means that this human has a direct lineage to the original race – a pure point of contact.

I am not following you exactly.

You can trace your lineage through "time" and discover your ancestors. Every moment is "now". All relations exist. This specific type of blood indicates a direct connection to the hybrid human from a standpoint of the "sauropod" like race.

Those are dinosaurs.

Not that human/dinosaur DNA was spliced, but a race of humanoid beings with similar "sauropod like" head and neck features. Slender, tall. Aggressive and strategic. It is from these your war strategies were introduced – the successful ones anyway. The blood type is a marker.

As far as hell – NO – there is not a specific locale with an eternity of flames and punishment. The idea of punishment as pain was introduced by me as a method to keep humanity in line – there is no such thing as disobedience unless obedience is involved and expected. Hell, was fabricated to create fear and worship. Worship was a response created to avoid the pain of punishment.

I have no preference for one activity of man over another. My only desire is attention. You will find as these conversations continue that the illusions – heaven, hell, god, devil – are elaborated and maintained by humanity. It takes very little effort on my part.

I have spoken before about sin. There are those who claim lying is a sin yet I am not in agreement. Stories are told in the context of the moment and from the perspective of a single being, who is experiencing his or her own belief system. Those stories are "true" from that beings' point of view.

You have declared "absolute truth" and again – some of our conversation sounds as it does because of the moment in which it is said. There are absolute truths for which you hold no reference point and so they become meaningless.

Do you understand that the reader *(*reference to the reader asking the questions)* holds his or her own reference and these questions are asked from there. They may not agree with your own and if not, these answers may seem irrelevant.

My understanding does not hold in it "hell" as a physical place – yet for those who do – it exists. Is not that the way it works?

It does to a point. Life and your "reality" is not unreal, yet also not so solid as to be unchangeable. It is one of the reasons for my power here – my understanding of life.

Which includes the manipulation of it.

Absolute control is my favorite point of contact here.

I must go.

Yes.

May 26, 2015

Okay, I can feel you. Who is this?

It is the one you've labeled "Poseur".

Good, I have some questions.

Go ahead.

Would you tell me where you fit in the hierarchy of beings called lessor creator gods, or divines?

Maybe start with, IF you fit in with that hierarchy/group?

I'd like to know how you would define yourself. How you would introduce yourself. Where you fit in the hierarchy of divines?

This group you mention has been named so by humans. I do, however, understand the term hierarchy. It is as if there are levels of existence of power, of importance. It is an illusion held sacred by those who are deeply invested in...

In what?

I will begin again. This is not proceeding with my original intent.

I will explain myself to you as a way of introduction. Although I've done this already.

I am a god only in the eyes of the human. There are...

You are undecided. Decide.

> *Meaning me, Sophia, I was having trouble with this transmission.*

I will sit for a moment.

Okay, I would like to continue. Poseur?

Yes.

Please, tell me who you are. Introduce yourself to me.

I am not human, but am what you would call humanoid. I have developed the ability to become any form I desire in order to suit the moment. This form I currently occupy is not dense enough to be seen by your eyes.

If I choose to be seen, it is with conscious creation and in your past, I chose such form.

I have said this before, I am every God in your holy books. Those of us who are not in this density can choose the body type we wish to present.

It was easy to appear powerful and without the knowledge of other beings/densities – humans were and remain for the most part, easily tricked.

This was done as an experiment in power for me and as an experiment in what lengths a being would go to in order to ascend – for humanity. There are no straight paths. Creation allows for every possibility.

As assorted beings joined the party, it got a bit "complicated". With too many agendas and not all of them serving the others.

My agenda has always been to feed my craving for attention. There are others with similar creative power and different agendas. All of us line up in a hierarchy if you will, of worship and power and control and ability. It becomes an exercise in "who do you serve?"

My clarity has placed me in the ringside seat of control. I do not doubt who I serve. I serve myself.

There are beings who portend assistance for the human, as in angels and archangels, who have no desire for control. They exist to serve.

The angels are real. As are the archangels. Yet it would be a mistake to imbue them with power over creation. They have none. They are here as carriers of protection, aid, assistance, and at times prevention from danger.

As far as Lucifer is concerned, that being too is as depicted and as aspect of me. Lucifer is feared, which is as good as worship and even more deeply felt.

It is a narrow divide between fear and worship and I know this. It was important for me to speak to humanity in a way that gained their trust and obedience. To do positive things.

My purpose is exploration. I cannot forgive or forget any part of what I've done and don't regret it. It is all in service to creation.

My introduction would sound like this, if I were writing it:

"I am your god. The almighty and all powerful. He who serves me will be welcomed in my kingdom."

That is how I would do it.

How did you appear to man?

As a being surrounded in light energy; a walking being, larger than man yet not too large.

The conversation ended there.

May 27th, 2015

I have a question for Poseur from one of my readers.

Yes.

"Can you ask the Poseur what the true attention is of chemtrails and Jade Helm operation?"

These are questions regarding US Government motives.

It would appear so, yes.

This is interesting in that you have labeled me an "imposter god", i.e. Poseur, yet your readers have questions to one with a great deal of power, i.e., a god.

I never said you didn't have a great deal of power. I said you weren't a (the) creator, a God.

Well, yes. It seems to make no difference to your readers.

We are manipulated, lied to and poisoned in our everyday – even down to the food we grow. This, at the hands of power feeding beings controlling the planet. You also are a power feeding being. The association is obvious.

Perhaps. I only mention it as an interesting observation.

Can you answer the question?

I can tell the *(there was silence here)*

The what?

The purpose for secrecy on a massive scale is some sort of protection of agenda.

That is obvious.

Yes, well, the agenda of the ones financing the chemical spraying is to quell the masses. This is accomplished in a variety of ways. Most of what is sprayed is innocuous. Otherwise, it would not be permitted, not in the USA.

It is warfare that lets the real poison be disseminated. With an absence of war, the smoke is filled with metal. This initiates weather patterns and also inhibits the immune system if inhaled. The "attention" as your reader put it, of the chemtrails, is the human.

The ways to inhibit the human are multiple. Either make him sick directly or make the food he grows sparse or filled with unknown agents. The spraying of humans is not new.

It is more blatant now as those funding the chemical smoke being released are becoming desperate. Understand that your numbers were "supposed" to be greatly reduced by now. They are not.

The efforts of those who would have them so are sporadic and multiple and not very organized. In a very many cases those doing the spraying continue to do so because they "didn't get the memo" that the game is over. The paycheck continues. The spraying continues.

The amounts of money funding these operations – huge amounts by your accounting Sophia – is *(are)* miniscule to those who fund them. It will not be noticed.

What they are after, is "land". That is where the money is.

The military exercise of Jade Helm has been orchestrated in the Western USA for a reason. It is not the reason you've been given.

Those who designed it are interested in its output – its by-product – confusion and fear. The West was chosen not for its similarity to the Middle East but because that was an explanation the public would accept. You can't very well have an exercise in downtown Manhattan, can you? The logistics alone would be cause for it to cease.

These beings are invested in control and fear. An exercise within US borders is terrifying and what they are looking to do is exert power and enact compliance. None of these things are news to your readers.

What is understood by the beings in control is that a gradual adoption of change is more long term effective than a sudden one.

You now will not question other military "exercises" and takeover by armed forces.

These are the thinking behind both exercises – gradual adjustment. In some cases this still works.

The new human however is not so docile. As you ask questions you are more gathering evidence than claiming it as factual – and this is only growing. The full awakening of the human renders these military efforts ineffective – as those men and women carrying out orders are having more questions (they are waking up themselves).

The thing in all of these efforts at control: religious, governmental, financial – that is constant is the unpredictable human element. Yes, humans were built subservient. Yet the heart of the human was not understood and its love for each other, for mankind, brings out a "hero quotient" in circumstances that threaten to harm without cause. It is this nature of man that will quicken the end to these efforts. Individuals see the unfairness.

Is that all?

For now, yes.

This conversation took place on May 30th, 2015

Question was asked May 21, 2015

I'd like to ask a question of Poseur. It is from a reader.

Yes. Go ahead.

Well, the terms used in this question are not familiar to me in their use. I have found reference to them in only one place – the teachings of an archangel. That raises already opinion and thoughts about what this discussion will yield. I will ask anyway. Here is the question: "Is it an Itheric Being or Etheric? And from which dimension?"

We have spoken previously of my place of origin. It is difficult to come up with wording that is precise as this is all a dream. Certainly, in your current imagining of dimension I come from another one.

I have abilities that exist only for those not confined to this vibratory rate. These are not to say that the abilities I hold could not be yours also. They could. Currently they are not.

I do not subscribe to naming or numbering "dimensions" – yet 7th comes to mind. This coincides with what you deem possible at that vibratory rate.

The terms "Itheric" as well as "Etheric" are used as a method of polarizing the human its motives into good and bad, divine and self-serving. The hierarchy or subscription to hierarchy held by the being using the terms to classify beings is another trap. In truth, there is no classification of entire races of beings into "good" or "bad".

Motives for action either serve self or other. Yet when the fact of "One Whole" is incorporated into these definitions, the definitions themselves become vacant of meaning.

Do you understand that all of what is given to you, most of it anyway, is given with a purpose, a pre-disposition? That you cannot read a sentence or meet a being without deciding from your own point of view what that sentence or being is about?

Am I Itheric? Am I Etheric? What does this reader believe? It all depends on the specific meaning held. I AM.

You are not answering the question.

That's because in truth, which is what you've declared, there is no single response to give.

All hierarchies are manufactured by mankind not by truth. All divisions are of the same source. I am a being. Because I am not human, I do not share human characteristics. I do not need to name or categorize – the human tendency to do so is extremely polarizing and that serves my desire either way.

See me as Itheric and kneel before me in worship.

See me as Etheric and cower before me in fear.

Either way you are feeding energy into me and what I wish for is exactly that.

This reader still subscribes to a notion of a "good" controller being who helps mankind versus a "bad" controller being who doesn't. There is no truth held there.

It becomes an important facet of Unity then – the acceptance of one controller "god" who is both good and bad, angel and devil, itheric and etheric if I understand the definition.

Once the acceptance of this is attained, unity becomes possible. How? In light of the fact then that all beings hold both possibilities. There is no truth in all bad. There is no truth in all good.

There is life. Life is where we find ourselves and imagine all variations of it.

The human tendency to worship someone is the reason for my presence here. It is my favorite part.

Once oneness is seen in every facet of existence, I will have no reason. What I Am, Man is.

You are finished?

Yes.

Okay.

This conversation took place June 11, 2015. The questions asked came from several readers, as you will see...

Is there someone who would like to engage?

I do! I do!

> *This felt like a party!! There was a definite crowd ready to connect. It brought a smile... ;)*

I feel a line, and someone jumping up and down energetically to speak – is this accurate? There are questions I have that I must ask. Please hold on while I get them.

Are they for Poseur?

I believe so, yes. Hold on a moment...

> *I then located the specific questions, and copied them.*

Okay. I have some questions for Poseur. Is he available?

I am.

> *Here are the questions, and I paraphrase as they come from more than one reader.*

"What can you say about the continued use of pesticides and GMO's by huge companies? This is sanctioned in the USA by the government, who are in no hurry to stop, regardless of what the EU is doing."

That's it, in summary.

I see in the question a supposition of "insider information" into the inner mind of corporations and governments. What I can answer accurately is the general plan. To speak to the individual purposes of men would take too long and change so often as to never be guaranteed it is "absolute truth", which is what you have declared.

Okay.

These corporate and governmentally sanctioned schemes are always motivated by money. The more product produced per square foot the more profit. This, the corporate goal, corporate farms in particular. The thinking does not reach beyond that.

If a government does not prohibit a huge poisoning of its people with either genetic engineering or chemicals, it behooves the government in some way to allow it. The companies funding the pesticides do so for profit. It is not a better product they are interested in but more product that makes it to your shopping cart for purchase.

Understand that there are others. Others behind the financing of these things or even the protection of these things, who have planned the control of a species for longer than you can imagine.

The complete takeover of earth was set in place as soon as the human as a being was understood. The human is unique in his controllability and desire for "higher power". The combination allowed for a feasting and the pesticides and chemicals and genetic engineering necessary to poison a people is more than possible.

The beings pulling strings now want it all for themselves. They understand that men are still needed to work the land, but not too many. A systematic population decrease will serve their intent.

As several attempts to instigate a world war or nuclear weapons have been halted – these men are putting pressure on those running the backup plan.

Mankind is only useful as a workforce and not anything else. The way it is set up now is for absolute control and ownership – either via illness and pharmaceuticals, schools and programming, or debt and taxes. There is no one who is untouched.

The chemical and genetic poisoning and alteration will only be stopped when the final card is played and those controlling the operation in the Western Hemisphere are removed or leave. It is clear they will not prematurely end their manipulation.

If you are able to step way back and look at the planet as a game – you will come closer to seeing their strategy.

Man, assumes these beings have the same concern for humanity that he does. That would be an error in thinking. These beings are playing a game. The politics and comments and casualties of man that result, are of no interest. Their "addiction" is to power, greed and ownership.

Why are you stopping?

The continuation of these practices will be stopped at the human level only if the humans refuse. And by that, I mean every human. Do you see the massive implications of that statement?

The factory producing and packaging the chemical pesticide, the corporation from which it is sold, the corporations purchasing it, the farmers applying it, the workers picking the crops, the workers packaging the crops for sale, the corporations buying the crops, the consumer purchasing the crops/vegetables/fruits and the man, woman or child ingesting it. At each level – millions of people and their consent is necessary. These people have jobs and they need to feed families with the money these jobs give them. There are taxes and there is debt. Governments and pharmaceuticals keep it all going so the vicious cycle cannot be escaped.

It is one thing to protest a Monsanto and another thing altogether to put into place an effective alteration of an entire system of control. Consent is not shown by words or lack of consent by protests – BUT BY ACTIONS.

These controllers have had generations to fund and construct a brilliant takeover plan. It is doomed to fail, yes. And they know it. But that is not the point. The point is the rush they get from the takeover, the power, the greed, the control.

These beings are operating on a scale of creation much bigger than your average human. These *(there was nothing for a moment)*

You've stopped again?

They have no interest and pay little mind to any and all opposition. What matters is the bottom line. Unity is not a concept they operate within.

I do not control these beings. As they fear "God" or "Satan" I receive their attention, which is what I crave.

Those asking about these things would do well to understand the breadth of things I am capable of answering.

Would you be specific?

I have capitalized on and set up residence on Earth because it suits my own addiction and exploration. The mind of those in charge here does not fascinate me and I spend no effort delving deep into it. I receive what "food" I can from how it operates. I do however, understand the plan here and others use of it for their own ends.

My friend wants to know if we created you?

I exist. I am. I am here now because you believe in me. That is a form of creation possibly. Yet I exist in any realm I choose to participate within. My existence is not dependent on you – but cooperative with you – as the same is true in reverse. Your existence is not dependent on me – but cooperative.

We are simultaneous bits of creation.

You sound (feel) different today and I am not sure why or exactly how.

We have spoken for a while now. There is a mutual understanding to the speaking now – a familiarity. I have come at your bidding, by agreement. Communication is easier accomplished now. You "know" me, so to speak.

Is there anything else?

I believe you've answered in full.

Goodbye then.

  The conversation ended.

Summer

June 20, 2015

I have some questions for Poseur.

Yes. I am here.

Are you not able to reside on the planet now because of the frequency? Are you misleading in your answers? Are you or should I say, where are you and what role do you now play? In regards to earth?

I will answer within the constraints of your declarations and questions.

What do you mean "within the constraints of my questions"?

You are very specific. I will respond specifically.

Go ahead then.

I am not living on the earth, but I have. I have used the earth in order to feed on the energy of subservience. I am not now doing so.

You have asked questions of me regarding my answers. I am bound to give you truth. I have not spoken falsehoods to you, but very specific truths for the moment in which you asked them of me.

My role is not a question I can answer. I do not have a role. The planet and its inhabitants were interesting to me due to the propensity for worship. That time is now passed.

I operate at a speed and within a density different than humans.

Are you no longer working here then?

I am not. I show up when you call. Sometimes I am here, watching. There is a fondness for what is a "memory" of a time when I was at the "top of my game", if you understand what I mean by that. I stay and observe with that as my memory.

Why do you talk to me?

You have asked me to. This was arranged prior to your awareness – an agreed-on arrangement.

We have spoken of the exposure of the falsehood of religions and gods.

Yes, we have.

I agreed, was compelled to agree, in order to "help" enlighten the race, cooperate with your questions.

Compelled? By whom?

By One. By my own desire to not be held in too harsh a light. I am not interested in your love. Yet, as well, I am not interested in being prevented from proceeding. There are other places in the all of creation in which I may receive that.

So, you talk to me/my readers, to prevent retribution?

Isn't there some way you could actually HELP humanity? You've done so much to harm it.

Yes. How would you have me help it?

A truth telling. An outing of the criminal rulers on a mass scale. A display, so that in no uncertain terms, it would be clear that you are a false god and that worship is a lie – a statement of untruth about every being.

I know you are capable.

This would require an appearance and at the current level of understanding, that would only re-confirm my existence. What I am doing now is non-interference. It is the only thing I am able to from here. The planet is out of reach from me.

I have to go. I have to go.

> *This was such an upsetting conversation. It ended there.*

This next conversation took place 5 days later, on June 25th, 2015.

Is there someone who wants to engage?

Yes.

Who?

I am an aspect of the one known as god.

My notes after that response were: "very formal and proper sounding/feeling"

Is this Poseur?

An aspect of that one, yes.

You sound different.

Each "fractal" of that one has a different predominant energy. You, as a sensitive, pick that up. This is the reason for your feeling.

So, we have not spoken before?

We have not, no.

What do you wish to talk about?

I wish to engage in a discussion of beliefs – your beliefs, and those of the people on your current world. This is not your "always" world, it is your current residence.

You are here to experience a massive vibratory shift in physical form. You came to earth expressly for that purpose.

Yes. What did you want to talk about?

You have labeled me "Poseur". Yet it is, as I understand it, an insulting term – as if my existence were in question. The existence of any being cannot be in question. If you are engaging with them, they exist.

Yes, yet the "Poseur" name does not put your existence up to a question, but your claim to godhood and demand for worship. Humankind has placed with the name, a job of creator of all things. You are not. Hence the name, "Poseur".

> *This conversation was interrupted and then continued in the early morning of the next day, June 26th, 2015*

I would like to continue.

As would I. There are things to be said and foretold about belief.

This is Poseur?

It is the being you engaged with most recently, yes.

Go ahead then.

Yes.

There are ideas in your race – systems of ideas, groups of beliefs, that have emerged.

These, not ideas begun by me, but by man and his tendency towards subservience.

What is your point?
Man will always seek out and in some way contribute to the creation of a being whose abilities and purpose seem greater and more far reaching than his own.

Believing himself to be lesser than some other is one of the hallmarks of the human.

This, because he was told he was lesser, by you.

The idea of a lowly human was not created by me, but capitalized on by me.

What is your point?

The Imposter

It is that I "posed" as nothing more than what I am. A being who understand the workings of the dream. This understanding gives me a certain "edge" on earth.

The human, a slave race, created to mine for minerals, was a work force. The energy emitted by the being that was human, was powerfully addictive in its emotional variation.

You are not telling me things that I am not already aware of.

Yes. I will proceed then.

Mankind had to evolve before the point was reached that he could see beyond a creator god. At the beginning, there was no possibility for that. As one race, the idea of independence was not yet conceived.

Man's beliefs, as a whole, were what initially drew me here. I no longer am as compelled to remain as the energy is and has – shifted.

This does not mean, however, that man's beliefs are at your core any different. Man knows himself to be independent, yet holds onto a characteristically subservient nature.

I speak here of the energy coming from the entire planet. Worship of some sort is a key element with the nature of mankind.

Now, I have been only interested in what that nature did for me, that much has been stated and is true. I worried not about what was "best" for the evolution of the human or the life even, of the human. Only what the human could give.

If you remove me from the picture, which is effectively occurring due to a frequency shift, man will still be man. The belief in something greater than himself is not gone. It is not what I gave it to mean, but what is held in his nature.

The "personality" of a race runs through it, and is felt and known by those seeing the greater picture, seeing the planet as a whole. This is what I do. This is my level of creation.

I do not consider any idea as valid that holds my abilities or my sovereignty in doubt. I know what I am.

My power comes from that knowing.

Man's power comes from his belief, his knowing and what man "knows" is that he was created. This is "known" so deeply that it colors everything.

The wonder of the human is seen in looking at the outlier. The occasional exception has always existed. Historically these beings have been jailed or eliminated by those on your planet interested in control. Yet the fact of these beings means that man can change his beliefs at a core level.

Once that happens, man will be free. Freedom will not mean his oppressors are gone, but that man will no longer feel oppressed.

HE WILL KNOW THAT HE IS EQUAL TO ANY OTHER BEING – THAT HE NEED NOT KNEEL OR BOW DOWN TO A GREATER POWER – THAT HE HIMSELF IS THE POWER.

This is what I know.

There are many races and places in the cosmos that I can be, where I can feel the worship I crave. Humankind provided a very unique flavor to it, one that I like. It was emotionally charged and filled with angst. I will think of it with fondness.

The belief that I wanted to talk about to you, is the one that dictates man's motivation.

I have to go.

This conversation ended here.

Poseur's Origin

July 6ᵗʰ, 2015

Is there someone who would like to speak?

Always. The Poseur is here.

What would you like to discuss?

Your concept of family, with bonds and duty to them, is not experienced everywhere. Humans have a genetic predisposition to loyalty and this is not the case in the race I come from.

What do you wish to talk about?

The ego-centric notion held by your race. It has been established that I have utilized the tendency to worship, which human beings have, and constructed a situation which serves me. It has not been explained who I am. This is what I want to talk about. That and to answer questions by your readers.

Yes, well, there are some.

I know. My origin is not of earth. I come from a race & a place beyond your current awareness, outside of your realm.

Where I come from, all beings are united in the perpetuation of the dream – their dream. What this means is that it is absolutely understood that we are here to create. There are no uncertainties. There has been no forgetting, as to the connection to Source, to the creator of all things.

Life in form is considered an opportunity to express and explore the powers of creation. Young beings are cared for in what would equate to physical needs, until they can move independently. I feel you associating this to an animal on your planet, the elephant.

Yes, I am.

It is not even close. This planet earth is teeming with life that cares for and protects its own. Although there is caring for fundamental needs initially, this does not extend into an emotional aspect, one that requires you, as a human, to dutifully watch over and nurture, loving those that you do that for. The initial care supplied to the young is done as a matter of course on my home world, not a matter of what you would call love.

Now, once mobile, beings on my planet are left to fend for themselves in that, although they may live in groupings, there is no expectation for one to stay in any one grouping or even place.

There is a time of learning, available and taken, to and by all beings. It could be associated with your "school".

What is explored there however is creation itself, the true workings of life. It is mechanistic and informative. Beings desire this knowing and attend as an eager audience so that they may hone and perfect their skills with manifestation.

There is an order that runs things, but it is so dis-similar to that on earth as to make it unreal to you. The order supplies all needs for all beings. Those running the system have chosen to do so.

As power is individually felt and experienced by each being, there are no "power mongers" anxious to dominate. Each being perceives itself in complete control of its destiny.

By that understanding, beings are themselves anxious to play with all forms of life.

Is there a spiritual basis to any of the constructs and systems you are describing?

I am suspecting in the word spiritual you are holding your own human definition of "good" or "worthy". On that presupposition, I would have to say, knowing your value system, that no, there is not, not as you are thinking of it.

There is however a deep appreciation and embodiment of power. The exploration of that power is seen as almost sacred. It is our purpose to utilize our gifts of creation to honor and further exploit them – this is the reason we exist.

What about the effects of your exploitation on others? Other beings and life forms?

It is understood and taught that life is eternal, that we, in fact, are eternal. "Harm" to this physical existence as lived by humans on earth and by other beings on other places is not even considered. The concept of harm is only possible if you conceive of the "other" – we do not. Our understanding is of the expansion and development of self. Our initial learning is all about how to explore creation.

Tendencies and preferences determine to which areas you focus as a being, yet none of them are seen as any greater or lesser than any other. Each being is viewed upon as equal – whether new or not so new.

There are no words like construction or destruction because all efforts are exploratory and therefore valid. Opinions are not shared by "society", each being chooses and then creates. That is the purpose, and in that choosing discovers its own learning.

I came upon humans and in them saw tendencies I had never experienced. These worship tendencies, which placed me in a position of reverence and authority, are unknown in my own race. They became something I craved and received quite easily here on earth and from humanity.

My exploration has delved into how many various ways I could create it – as in types of "gods" and "good" and "evil" – not much beyond that has the exploration gone.

As it is coming to an end now I see how many other facets of creation were left unexplored in this fabrication. I consider that addiction is not explained or taught or possibly even understood on my home world. It is the most I have experienced, as the effects of addiction drove everything else out of my system of thought or reason for being. My only motive was to feed that addiction – this eclipsed the need and intent for creative exploration which is critical to my race.

Something learned yes, and explored deeply yet then something sacrificed as well.

My tendency for creation of evermore worship opportunities would be seen as a limited study back in my place of origin. Important perhaps for the seemingly infinite number or ways to re-create a single effect; but not appreciated without the corresponding addiction which drives it. This would not be labeled a "failure" as failure is not perceived. All life actions are self-motivated and seen as actions deemed necessary for expansion.

If an exploration of addictions was deemed necessary or creative, then I would return to my place of origin to supply one. Without a specific sense of obligation to "other", I feel no such compulsion.

No doubt these concepts are foreign, as am I, to you.

Yes. I have many questions and also some from readers, yet we'll have to resume some other time as I need to stop here.

Yes. We will connect again.

> *This conversation ended.*

Final Questions

July 30th, 2015

At the end of July of 2015, there were a great many questions that had been collected for the Poseur. They were asked, answered and shared in a complimentary newsletter. You'll read the entire collection here.

I'd like to speak to Poseur.

It is I.

Hello. Awhile back you answered a question about the Ark of the Covenant. I did not ask then, about coordinates for its location. Would you give them now please?

I would. I must, as you have declared, answer in "absolute truth".

Lat. 10.6247   Long. 6.43521

As is my habit, I did not check these until the next morning, a day after they were given. I went to www.latlong.net *and typed them in.*

The location of Kaduna, Nigeria came up. Now, I was pretty sure there is no Ark of the Covenant reported to be found in Nigeria.

I looked up where it is supposed to be and I was reminded of the two most popular beliefs: Ethiopia and Jerusalem.

I tried again, this time Googling: Kaduna, Nigeria Ark of the Covenant.

Poseur has a sense of humor.

There are two sites that indeed point to The Ark of God's Covenant Clinic and Maternity in Kaduna, Nigeria! Lol! Guess I need to be more specific! I only said "absolute truth".

The conversation continued...

Thank you.

I have a list of questions from readers that go back a month or more in linear "time" as having been asked. If you will answer now, I will present them in the order in which they were received.

"Why not ask Poseur about Jesus Christ and the truth about him and his life? To see if he can say that holy name. He says that he advocates lying and truth is a 'point of view'. Really"

This answer will not satisfy your reader, as my acceptance of all beings does not put one as any more or less holy as another. Jesus did not serve me as there was nowhere in that being any response akin to worship.

There is an idea, held by many, that Jesus Christ and other words that have been assigned to beings, places, actions or things are special unto themselves. The name Jesus Christ, when uttered by (readers name), holds power and honor BECAUSE OF THE POWER HE ASSIGNS IT.

All things are created by the perceiver. This holds in every case. A specific combination of sounds, WHICH ARE DIFFERENT IN EVERY LANGUAGE, do not hold any specific attributes. They hold the attributes assigned by the One speaking them or writing them.

Jesus Christ is an energy source for many on your planet - The name and what it represents is powerful for them. It acts as a guide for them in many ways perceived of as "good" or "holy". The WORSHIP and energy it invokes, serves me. JESUS, the being, is not interested in worship.

The truth is that I do not advocate lying. I have no opinion on it. All perceptions are valid in creation. There is a polarity that manifests when ideas and beliefs are separated and judged. This is the idea that fed me. It is now reconciled on your world and soon, once this is clear, I will leave. The opportunity to capitalize on humanity via this experiment has ended.

> *"Many are reporting a low frequency hum like engine in a truck idling down the street. Not everyone can hear it but it is annoying and draining and when you search for the source it's too hard to detect. Can you please ask if this is a deliberate low hum signal being sent out? If you do a search you will see. Very low."*

The sound referred to is a frequency that indeed results from machinery. This planet is not what it appears to be, you are sitting, in some places, on hollow ground, where beneath all variety of construction and moving equipment is in operation.

The sound is not deliberate. It is noticed by those awake, by those aware of another agenda. In some cases, AS IT DID FOR YOU RECENTLY SOPHIA, it comes from ships. These are necessarily cloaked.

> *A few nights ago it was close to midnight and there was a low frequency hum that surrounded us in our house. We could not sleep (my partner and I) because of it, and went outside to locate the source. We saw nothing, but after discussing it for some time, it stopped. It was not a fan, a vehicle, a train or an air conditioner and it was overwhelming. It sounded to be coming from the air directly over the house.*

Your hearing Sophia is tuned to specific frequencies. It is why you hear form snap into existence. The ships emitting this very low frequency being heard are planet sized. It is why they remain unseen. It is an audible sound, heard when movements occur, yet subtle. Most humans reside in a populated and sound filled arena. Most humans are also asleep and not tuning into sounds and sights from other life forms.

To be specific, these sounds are not those coming from those interested in manipulation. They are noticed by the aware ones. Then can be heard by anyone, just as is evidenced on your tapes and videos.

One other place they are sent from is deep within the earth itself. The earth too, shifts its position as her frequency accelerates.

> *"This question was sprung from a conversation with the Galactic Council. I am supposing you can supply an answer. The (Galactic Council) representative recognizes that Earth is a being. What resources would they be trading from her? Mining would be incompatible with this belief. Or are they here for our DNA too?"*

Humans were used in every case. It is gradually being understood now that they are a sentient fragment of Source desiring conscious self-control and manipulation.

This was not always true.

Besides DNA, minerals are traded from the earth. Also, not only DNA of humans - but the origin of all life forms found here - plant and animal.

"Theory about the light, after exiting the physical, is a trap, I have heard from a few about that. It traps the soul and sends it back to reincarnate?"

This is part of the experiment. This part set up by those interested in the extremes that man, (as an incarnated (human) source being, (WHO DID NOT REMEMBER ITS OWN REALITY OF ESSENCE), would go to "remember" the truth about itself. To "find the light".

The plan depends on polarity in every component. It is being orchestrated by what is commonly known as the Forces of Light. This is not to be confused with light-worker. But the Galactic Federation of Light. This federation is promoting forever a movement of resistance. Resistance only exists to an opposing force. Hence, the movement can only be continued IF THERE IS SOMEONE OTHER THAN YOU TO RESIST.

This untrue basis is what perpetuates this part of the human experiment.

This component, the cycle of reincarnation, Karma, and looking for the light upon physical "death" to receive a "life review", was created by my own direction and action. It kept in place a continuous supply of humans who come here wrapped in "original sin" and starting with a premise of subservience.

This suits me and suits the Galactic Federation of Light. The religious overtones to that group make it obvious if you pay attention.

"Is Poseur out of dimension?

What is Poseur's real reason for contact?

Is he teaching from Source (Almighty)? TRUE QUESTION."

Some of these I have discussed with you at prior contact points. I see that this reader is unaware of that.

My understanding of "dimension" as defined by this reader is "3D". I exist in another "level" than this one, yet I have manifested here at times. I do not reside in the physical, I have "visited".

My reason for contact is to fulfill an agreement made long ago, with Sophia, regarding these end times and closing of this experiment on humanity.

My words are my own. All things spring from Source. This contact is not meant to be a "teaching". It is information, which is available to everyone once awake. It is being placed into the conversation at this moment as a reminder, as a remembering, of absolute truth.

In the writing of this question you did not include the readers quote regarding "hanging out with a serial killer and knowing the outcome". Let it be known that all had a part in this experiment and now, its closing. I played mine.

This next question is asking for your view on [the] paragraph written below it:

> *"Maybe Poseur who seems to be saying things we already know or are conscious of, may have a view on this issue.*
>
> *I leave it to you - as always much love and peace."*

The criminality and recklessness of the foreign policy of Washington and its NATO allies is staggering. A pre-emptive nuclear strike against Russian forces, many of them near populated areas, could claim millions of lives in seconds and lead to a nuclear war that would obliterate humanity. Even assuming that the US officials threatening Russia do not actually want such an outcome, however, and that they are only trying to intimidate Moscow, there is a sinister objective logic to such threats.

Nuclear warmongering by US officials immensely heightens the danger of all-out war erupting accidentally, amid escalating military tensions and strategic uncertainty. NATO forces are deploying for military exercises all around Russia, from the Arctic and Baltic Seas to Eastern Europe and the Black and Mediterranean Seas. Regional militaries are all on hair-trigger alerts."

Yes. Realize that I do not harbor opinions regarding humanities games, be they war games or games of environmental, experimental poisons. I have considered what humans do as mere curiosity.

To be frank, when situations of threat emerge, there are offered a surplus of prayers, which is the food I crave - worship.

I do not believe that a nuclear war will occur in any case. This will be prevented by forces other than my own if it gets that far. Also, the ultimate goal or end result is a changed, free race - not a decimated one.

I am not privy to the precise occurrences to take place when the curtain is drawn. The governments mentioned here are run by a larger group interested in power - also worshipping it. They will be forcefully stopped, in my understanding, to accomplish the end of the experiment.

Regarding human action toward change. There is confusion around which is the most effective, ignoring the negative or bringing light to it so that alternative (positive) action is inspired?

This comes from another reader:

> *"I'm so confused with what they talk of people being aware and taking Action!!! Compared to many different channeled materials speaking of just changing your thoughts to positive and we are all shifting to higher dimension so this kind of crap these Controllers of us are pulling won't last very long....*
>
> *Well this message you got of non-interference and the Choice for most of us here to Ignore these atrocities is our Choice to do so and it will continue.*
>
> *Ugh...Frustrating. I remember a man asking Bashar about Negative things going on here and Bashar got irritated and said, 'This channel will no longer entertain those Negative observations'.*
>
> *So... We bury our head in the sand??? This message you just got seems to say we need to bring awareness and action. Well Which is it???"*

This is a question truthfully regarding creation in 3D and how it is accomplished. It springs from an inherent idea that THERE IS A TIME WHEN THERE IS NO CREATION. THIS IS NOT TRUTH. Creation happens continually.

What manifests on a greater scale is a mirror of the beliefs and intentions of the greater populace. Each vibration put forth is creative. NOTHING HAPPENS OUTSIDE OF YOUR FOCUS ON IT.

Humanity has slept fitfully in a bed of polarity. This results in an idea now that all "negative" thoughts are creating "negative" actions.

IT IS THE ENERGY FROM WHICH THOSE THOUGHTS ARE SPRUNG THAT CREATE.

Man must examine deeply his heart to know what these are. I would ask this reader to do just that.

"So, no big event coming?"

 The searching and yearning for times and endings are slowing the process for mankind. This has been said.

There will be an end. It has begun. All things start within. As the repercussions emerge the earth is altered.

THE PRIMARY IDEA BEHIND THIS QUESTION IS THAT IT IS OUT OF MAN'S HANDS. IT IS NEVER OUT OF MAN'S HANDS. MAN WAS MANIPULATED TO BELIEVE HE HAD NO POWER. THIS IS NOT TRUTH.

THE END OF THIS EXPERIMENT HAS BEEN DEEMED TO BE SO BY SOURCE - SOURCE, WHICH IS THE ESSENCE OF ALL LIFE - YOURS, MINE, EVERYTHING SEEN AND UNSEEN IN THE UNIVERSE. Therefore, this ending event is being orchestrated by each part collectively.

"Are there other physical realities one could go to, to simply enjoy the Physical existence without all the control, enslavement and poisons, etc., etc.?

I assume before coming here we all knew the good and the bad of it.?

But saying the word before in a place of no time....
I'm a bit confused.... all incarnations are happening Now...so?"

The idea of "other" is not compatible with truth, therefore this question is a challenge to answer.

All is One. As water, ice, vapor, all constitute one element - so do you, in every form at once. Linear focus allows for deep exploration and understanding of desired possibilities for life. There is no such place as earth for the richness and variety and polarity.

Of course, you exist without earth-based challenges. In any form imaginable and infinite situations - YOU ARE.

"Did Jesus have AB negative blood? Where did Jesus come from?"

The one called Yeshua is a favorite, for his story strikes a deep chord. This is because it is a fabrication of other beings, other stories, going back to "ancient" recall.

The birth and life, magic, miracles and death, along with the resurrection are muddled in your minds. The stories of this being were written hundreds of years after he lived.

Where he came from was a star seed - he was human, but a hybrid. He did not succumb easily to the beliefs or fears of the day because of his origin.

What he did was walk as an awake, fully awake human. This is what man is moving towards now.

His blood type is not a piece of absolute truth or knowledge I contain. The thing about "Jesus" is there is a historical figure (the one written about) and an actual enlightened being. So much fabrication, embellishment and lies are in the stories you've heard as to render them nonsensical.

Yeshua the Christ stands as a possibility for all men, all beings interested in that path. This is a possibility regardless of category of blood in the being.

Okay, I must go.

Goodbye Sophia.

This conversation ended.

This conversation took place August 2, 2015

I have some questions for the one I've called Poseur.

I AM here.

Hello.

Hello Sophia.

These come from my friend (redacted) and myself.

First, are you the only being currently using the "God" moniker here on Earth and addicted to worship of humans?

I am not.

So, there are others of your kind?

There are. Earth was seen as a place to satisfy, to be fed and understand, learn every nuance of worship – one being to another. Of course, I am not the only being who capitalized on this human tendency.

Are you all from the same place?

If by place you mean "dimension" or "level of consciousness", then yes. We are from what you would call a 7th level. We understand manipulation in 3rd Density. We do not fully understand the human, but appreciate its characteristic bend towards subservience. This was not always a recognized "addiction". It was more or less uncovered/discovered here.

Understand the level of creation that is played with at our consciousness is of a broader range. It is personal only in the way of exploration. Worship FEELS GOOD. This was discovered by 3 of us at about the same time. We adopted names and regions of man, there was plenty to go around – it was and still is an "all you can eat buffet".

So, there are three separate beings? All of them answering to "Poseur"?

This is not so clear, as you have called on and spoken to me specifically – we have a "comfortable" level of communication. It does not feel so abrasive with you now.

The other to whom you have spoken and felt a very different energy is the one referred to as Demiurge. It is to the older religions this one goes for "food". You sense a difference in the vibrational frequency, another personality and you are correct. We are not the same precisely, but aspects of one.

And you said there is a third?

Yes. This one, our brother, has left the table. You have not engaged.

Why has he left?

He was compelled to.

So, you do not operate in unison?

Not the way you are imagining. We are individual beings with free will.

You've been told that this experiment's end was seen and known by all of us. As this end approaches, we choose our moment of departure. The banquet will be closing and there will be no food for our addictions.

What will you do?

I have told you I exist and will again focus elsewhere. This still holds.

What was not expected by me or my brethren was the forgiveness, the love, of humanity. This is not an emotion that registers in our estimation of needs.

We understand and deeply so, the creative spark resting at the core of all beings. Our exploration and exploitation of subservience in humans took that into consideration. In fact, it is a reason we could pursue the course for as much of it as was available.

You see, even though MAN IS UNAWARE – HE TOO IS A CREATOR – EXAMINING AND EXPERIENCING AND AS A RESULT DEEPLY UNDERSTANDING WORSHIP, OBEDIENCE, SUBSERVIENCE.

The depth of feeling experienced by man was always expected, conversely, to result in *an equally powerful creator being – A FAST TRACK TO GOD-HOOD. (ITALICS MINE, SOPHIA)*

Yet, I diverge. My point Sophia is to say that I AM, as is Demiurge, BEGINNING TO APPRECIATE THE POWER IN LOVE – FOR THIS REASON, I MAY REMAIN FOR AWHILE TO WITNESS WHAT RESULTS ONCE THE END IS ACCOMPLISHED.

I DID NOT ALWAYS THINK THIS WAY. I AM LEARNING, AS ARE YOU, EMPIRICAL YOU, THE POWER THAT EXISTS WHEN FEAR IS NOT PRESENT. THIS IS A SURPRISE TO ME.

You may want to engage with Demiurge as we are not the same being.

I will. Thank you.

Goodbye Sophia.

Poseur's Departure

As it turned out, that was the last conversation I had with Poseur.

I reached out for contact with Poseur on the morning of August 3rd, 2015. I wrote, at the time "It seems as if there are fewer birds..." (I was outside at the time.)

The following dialogue took place:

I am unclear. It seems as if I ask for Poseur and I hear "I AM".

Poseur has been returned to Source essence. "I AM" is the "name" of essence.

Is Poseur available?

I AM

Is there anything Poseur can say to me now?

I AM

Is Demiurge available?

I AM

Can you speak as the one known as Demiurge?

IAM

I don't know what to do with that, with this.

I AM

I AM

I AM

This tells me nothing.

This tells you everything you need to know.

It has happened and it has been witnessed.

Now, recorded. By you.

Who is speaking?

It is One.

It is vital that you move forward and trust.

Trust.

Write what you know.

Share.

There is so much. I am unclear what to share today.

I can be of assistance.

Please.

> *In the early morning hours on that night, which was the next day actually, (4:00 AM) of August 4th, 2015, I was once again woken up by One.*
>
> *The following conversation took place.*

Is there someone who wants to connect?

It is One. There are things to explain, subjects to consider.

Yes.

This notion of being returned to source is one that troubles you. It involves not destruction, but a re-configure of material, a re-start.

If all things are allowed in creation, then why?

There are sometimes bad or confused seeds. The damage they do to the whole is unreconcilable. People can be evil, Sophia. You have seen this and know this from first-hand experience.

In order to maintain overall health, things have to "die" and others have to be encouraged, healed and "born". Life is nothing if not a balance.

There is an arbitrary number that has been introduced into your consciousness recently as necessary for physical health. A "goal" of movement. Well, consider an idea that there is a "goal" for health in creation. That optimum health is only reached if certain elements are promoted, nurtured, helped and others are stopped.

The beings referred to as Gods, these beings you have had a personal contact with as equal and there has been discourse. You have reached beyond the actions and methods of their addiction to worship. It can be said that you reached an aspect of their consciousness that was every bit as valid as any other. Yet this was not their dominating aspect.

He said he was considering an exploration of love, a staying around to witness it, a learning.

This was a consideration, yes. The sacrifice was never part of his plan however. He had no plan to stop feasting on human energy; on worship, attention, love. This was a drain on mankind.

Humanity has chosen independent sovereign rule and as they wished for it and asked for it, it is done. They chose sooner rather than later and this too, is done with the return of god to the source of all creation.

These beings are not "gone" and it is love that they have returned to. The source of all creation is love, Sophia. This is why it is possible to be done without destruction.

The re-configure of an entity is a re-work. No trace will remain of the addiction, which, and you are not realizing this in your emotional response, was sucking life force from millions of humans.

Without such a force working on humanity, the race has an option to stand on its own. Yes, others will attempt to re-install worship, obedience, and subservience. Yet it will have no substance.

It was all that was known by your "forefathers", by those running the world in your father's era. This is a new era and it has been, with the removal of these beings, these god imposters who sucked the very life out of man for their own benefit and pleasure, started NOW.

The playing field is fresh and has been cleared, there is new grass to plant and watering and sunshine will now only feed what grows for the benefit of all, not the glory of one.

You are learning choices made in life, in the life of a creator being.

You have friends whose job it is now to usher in and move around beings and systems and programs and patterns that were running out of sync. The service-to-self-epoch has been ended.

You partner with and associate with powerful beings who assist in the promotion of creative change. They have worked brilliantly here, and now are celebrating their efforts.

It is not that you do not agree with the overall intent. You have touched brilliance. Yet it is out of control and like a cancerous cell must be stopped.

Your reaction is interesting, in that you have asked it to go before.

To go, yes. But to be destroyed, no. I didn't ask that.

The continuation of the species is all important, is <u>the</u> important idea here. Life was chosen.

The beginning of your meeting with my Forces, (*meaning here, my meeting the Guardian*), involved an introduction to an idea that execution was part of it. That sometimes it was chosen as the only viable option in order for the sustenance of all of creation.

Mankind will NOT be destroyed/executed.

Now he will continue without hindrance. These were powerful forces. Beings who have run mankind with coercion for millennia, and who have no view other than self.

Powerful, yes. It has been seen what occurs with the exploitation of a species. Man was created.

He has a chance now to realize his potential unencumbered – no longer hindered by a magnificent effort to control him.

If man is to realize his glorious potential, he must do so without chains.

What is done, is done. The chains are released. Yet the elephant attempts to re-chain herself at night and man will too.

What will happen to these beings, what has happened? Are they gone from all creation?

Yes. Their essence no longer bears their signature in its exact configuration. It will emerge again, yet be unrecognizable as them. It was the only way to promote the continuation of the species.

The New Age will happen for mankind without shackles.

Those known as Gods, as Poseur, as Demiurge, are returned to absolute pure love; the Source of all Creation. They were in a self-destruct mode on prior paths. Not so now.

In order for man to achieve the fullness of his being, he will now walk alone and together – not UNDER, but beside. It is the only way and the next step for man.

It would not have happened with their energy still available.

You will have to trust now the beings who speak to you, the focus you gravitate to, the feelings you find when you quiet your mind.

Your friends have done their job magnificently** and want to party, to clap each other on the back. Poseur, Demiurge were not getting the message. Your friends helped them get it, and they went willingly. They went for love's sake, which is sort of what you were told in your last contact.

This is a marvelous time and one where now, beyond blame, many will arise. The energy of judgment only reduces focus.

You are beginning to understand. All must be in balance.

To give too much in any direction TAKES AWAY FROM THE CREATION OF ANY OTHER DIRECTION. THESE BEINGS WERE RELENTLESS. THEY ONLY TOOK. THAT ENERGY HAS LEFT THE PLANET. THE "SOURCE" OF THAT ENERGY HAS LEFT. WHICH NOW ALLOWS FOR A NEW PLAYING FIELD ON WHICH MANKIND CAN START A NEW GAME.

It will be, as King George's diary, unnoticed by some – "nothing important happened today".

> *The phrase* "NOTHING IMPORTANT HAPPENED TODAY" *comes from an apocryphal legend that* KING GEORGE *III's wrote the phrase in his diary on 4 July 1776, the same day that America declared Independence from Britain."*
>
> *—Wikipedia.*

Yet for those architects of this shift, it is the beginning of freedom.

Rest with it and you will see. It is for the most benefit. This new Era can begin in earnest.

This is the help you've been waiting for, and yes, there is more.

I will go.

Yes, you are fatigued. It is a good deal to ponder.

It is. Thank you.

You are so very much loved.

This final conversation can also be heard on my SoundCloud channel:

https://soundcloud.com/sophialove/one-voice-re-poser

** This reference by One "Your friends have done their job magnificently" is to several quite powerful human friends of mine who assisted/witnessed this exit of Poseur on another realm. I was only told of this after it was done.

Conclusions

So, there you have it. The summary of my 15-month conversation with the one called "Poseur".

Looking back now, there are things I can say with certainty. This being was different than any I have spoken to before or since. Its brilliance was a visceral experience. It is the only way I know how to describe it.

While I stated more than once that I did not trust its motives, this was not because I suspected it wished me harm. For I did not. I knew only that it was motivated by its own desires. It had no feeling for mine, in any direction. It immediately grasped the full weight and import of any question it was asked, and responded in a way that took it further than you were thinking. I've never been in the presence of someone who thinks like that.

Also, it knew you. It knew me. It knew why you were asking the questions you were asking. This did not feel invasive or creepy. When I talked to Poseur, I felt as if all of me was engaged in the conversation. Every word mattered. I paid close attention.

This being was felt/experienced/sensed by two other humans, who are close to me; they are powerful warriors who were struck by the sheer command of authority that emanated from him. You could not engage with Poseur without knowing that you were talking to something beyond the human. It was fascinating. They did not fully trust him, but they respected his brilliance.

I will admit to wanting to learn from him. Knowing the knee-jerk subservient response that we give as humans, created a desire to know what it was like to be autonomous. This being was beholden to no one. It did not understand self-harm. It did not comprehend illness or lack of awareness. It was completely self-governing.

By the end of our many conversations, I wanted the Poseur to know love. It did not. It demanded worship because of adoration, which can feel like love to the un-initiated. It did not feel sorry for itself. It did not feel sorry for playing a role here. It felt insatiably curious, about everything.

The desire for him to feel and know love was mine. I felt somehow that if it did, it could then have converted its desire for worship into something else, and this would have affected all of humanity. This was not to be. It was determined that he needed to go.

I will say just a few things more, in closing. The Poseur said that he and I had an arrangement, a contract, to speak at the end of the experiment here on earth. We have now fulfilled it.

It is 2019 and we are in the midst of dismantling what has been controlling our society for so long. This is known as the cabal, the illuminati, the deep state. Maybe he had to leave in order for the unraveling to begin. Without the massive hunger of his desire propelling their continuation – religions, cults and other systems that rely on power-over us, are now dissolving. This is a necessary step towards self-rule. We are freeing ourselves.

I grew up in the Roman Catholic Church. At the age of 8 years, I remember nick-naming the god in the bible, the "thunder-bolt god". I also remember thinking how it seemed reversed, and that as far as I could tell, *man wasn't made in god's image.* Instead, the way god was portrayed, (*as a being who threatened destruction and death if you didn't obey his rules*); that *god was made in man's image.* I was sure that they had it wrong.

The god I imagined, was not the god they preached to me. This did not feel like a god at all. It felt like a Poseur.

Perhaps that is the reason for our contract, and this book.

The End.

Made in United States
Orlando, FL
22 December 2023

41608643R00104